ISBN 978-1-330-77191-4
PIBN 10103379

1 MONTH OF
FREE
READING

at

www.ForgottenBooks.com

By purchasing this book you are eligible for one month membership to ForgottenBooks.com, giving you unlimited access to our entire collection of over 700,000 titles via our web site and mobile apps.

To claim your free month visit:

www.forgottenbooks.com/free103379

Similar Books Are Available from
www.forgottenbooks.com

KING LEAR'S WIFE

AND OTHER PLAYS

"REMEMBER THE
LIFE OF THESE
THINGS CONSISTS
IN ACTION."

JOHN MARSTON: 1606.

KING · LEAR'S · WIFE THE ·CRIER·BY·NIGHT THE·RIDING·TO·LITH- END▾MIDSUMMER·EVE LAODICE·AND·DANAË PLAYS · BY · GORDON BOTTOMLEY

CONSTABLE & COMPANY
LIMITED ▾ ▾ ▾ LONDON

First published 1920

PRINTED IN GREAT BRITAIN.
LONDON: PRINTED AT THE CHISWICK PRE
TOOKS COURT, CHANCERY LANE

CONTENTS

NOTE.—*Throughout the stage-directions in the following pages the words " right" and " left" are used with reference to the actor's right and left, not the spectator's.*

BIBLIOGRAPHICAL NOTE

THE plays here collected were originally published separately at various dates during the past eighteen years, and are now brought together for the first time. The details of the previous issues, now for the most part out of print, are appended.

I. THE CRIER BY NIGHT. (1900.) Published by the Unicorn Press, London, 1902. 32 pp. Quarto, boards 500 copies.

II. MIDSUMMER EVE. (1901-2.) Printed and published at the Pear Tree Press, South Harting, near Petersfield, 1905, with decorations by James Guthrie. iv + 36 pp. Large post 8vo, boards. 120 copies.

III. LAODICE AND DANAË. (1906.) Printed for private circulation, 1909. iv + 26 pp. Royal 8vo, wrappers. 150 copies.

IV. THE RIDING TO LITHEND. (1907.) Printed and published at the Pear Tree Press, Flansham near Bognor, 1909, with decorations by James Guthrie. vi + 40 pp. Foolscap 4to, boards. 120 copies (20 of which had an extra plate and were hand-coloured.)

V. KING LEAR'S WIFE. (1911-13.) Published in "Georgian Poetry, 1913-1915," pp. 1 to 47. The Poetry Bookshop, London, 1915.

THE CRIER BY NIGHT, THE RIDING TO LITHEND, and LAODICE AND DANAE have been reprinted in the United States of America, the first in 1909, the second in two separate forms in 1910, the third in 1916.

KING LEAR'S WIFE

B

TO T. STURGE MOORE

THE years come on, the years go by,
    And in my Northern valley I,
Withdrawn from life, watch life go by.
But I have formed within my heart
A state that does not thus depart,
Richer than life, greater than being,
Truer in feeling and in seeing
Than outward turbulence can know;
Where time is still, like a large, slow
And lofty bird that moves her wings
In far, invisible flutterings
To gaze on every part of space
Yet poise for ever in one place;
Where line and sound, colour and phrase
Rebuild in clear, essential ways
The powers behind the veil of sense;
While tragic things are made intense
By passion brooding on old dread,
Till a faint light of beauty shed
From night-enfolded agony
Shews in the ways men fail and die
The deeps whose knowledge never cloys
But, striking inward without voice,
Stirs me to tremble and rejoice.

For twenty years and more than twenty
I have found my riches and my plenty
In poets dead and poets living,
Painters and music-men, all giving,
By life shut in creative deeds,
Live force and insight to my needs;
And long before I came to stand
And hear your voice and touch your hand
In that great treasure-house new-known,
Where in their tower above the Town
The masters of The Dial sit,
I loved in every word of it

Your finely tempered verse that told me
Of patient power, and still can hold me
By its authentic divination
Of the right knowledge of creation,
Its grave, still beauty brought to day
Tissue by tissue in nature's way,
Petal by petal sure to shew
Imagination's quiet glow
That burns intenseliest at the core.
And through that twenty years and more
I have been envious of your reach
In speaking form and plastic speech,
Your double energy of hand
That puts two arts at your command
While I must be content with one
And feel true life but half begun;
So that by graver as by pen
You can create earth, stars, and men,
And prove yourself by more than rime
A prince of poets in our time.

For these delights, and the delight
Of converse in a Surrey night
After the deep sound had lapsed by
Of ocean-haunted poetry,
For counsel and another zest
Added to beauty's life-long quest
I, in acknowledgment, would bring
The homage of an offering,
And, being too poor to reach the height
Of my conception or requite
Your greater giving equally,
I search in my capacity
And, by my self-appointed trade,
Find something I myself have made,
That here I offer. Let it be
A token betwixt you and me
Of admiration and loyalty.

February 29th, 1916.

PERSONS:

LEAR, King of Britain.
HYGD, his Queen.
GONERIL, daughter to Lear and Hygd.
CORDEIL, daughter to Lear and Hygd.
GORMFLAITH, waiting-woman to Hygd.
MERRYN, waiting-woman to Hygd.
A PHYSICIAN.
TWO ELDERLY WOMEN.

KING LEAR'S WIFE

The scene is a bedchamber in a one-storied house. The walls consist of a few courses of huge irregular boulders roughly squared and fitted together; a thatched roof rises steeply from the back wall. In the centre of the back wall is a doorway opening on a garden and covered by two leather curtains; the chamber is partially hung with similar hangings stitched with bright wools. There is a small window on each side of this door.

Toward the front a bed stands with its head against the right wall; it has thin leather curtains hung by thongs and drawn back. Farther forward a rich robe and a crown hang on a peg in the same wall. There is a second door beyond the bed, and between this and the bed's head stands a small table with a bronze lamp and a bronze cup on it. Queen HYGD, *an emaciated woman, is asleep in the bed; her plenteous black hair, veined with silver, spreads over the pillow. Her waiting-woman,* MERRYN, *middle-aged and hard-featured, sits watching her in a chair on the farther side of the bed. The light of early morning fills the room.*

MERRYN.

MANY, many must die who long to live,
    Yet this one cannot die who longs to die:
Even her sleep, come now at last, thwarts death,

KING LEAR'S WIFE

Although sleep lures us all half way to death. .
I could not sit beside her every night
If I believed that I might suffer so:
I am sure I am not made to be diseased,
I feel there is no malady can touch me
Save the red cancer, growing where it will.
> *Tahing her beads from her girdle she
> kneels at the foot of the bed.*
O sweet Saint Cleer, and sweet Saint Elid too,
Shield me from rooting cancers and from madness:
Shield me from sudden death, worse than two
    death-beds;
Let me not lie like this unwanted queen,
Yet let my time come not ere I am ready—
Grant space enow to relish the watchers' tears
And give my clothes away and calm my features
And streek my limbs according to my will,
Not the hard will of fumbling corpse-washers.
> *She prays silently.*
> KING LEAR, *a great, golden-bearded man
> in the full maturity of life, enters
> abruptly by the door beyond the bed,
> followed by the* PHYSICIAN.

LEAR.
Why are you here? Are you here for ever?
Where is the young Scotswoman? Where is she?

MERRYN.
O, Sire, move softly; the Queen sleeps at last.

LEAR, *continuing in an undertone.*
Where is the young Scotswoman? Where is
    Gormflaith?

KING LEAR'S WIFE

It is her watch. . . . I know; I have marked your
    hours.
Did the Queen send her away? Did the Queen
Bid you stay near her in her hate of Gormflaith?
You work upon her yeasting brain to think
That she's not safe except when you crouch near
    her
To spy with your dropt eyes and soundless
    presence.

MERRYN.
Sire, midnight should have ended Gormflaith's
    watch,
But Gormflaith had another kind of will
And ended at a godlier hour by slumber,
A letter in her hand, the night-lamp out.
She loitered in the hall when she should sleep.
My duty has two hours ere she returns.

LEAR.
The Queen should have young women about her
    bed,
Fresh cool-breathed women to lie down at her side
And plenish her with vigour; for sick or wasted
    women
Can draw a virtue from such abounding presence,
When night makes life unwary and looses the
    strings of being,
Even by the breath, and most of all by sleep.
Her slumber was then no fault: go you and find
    her.

PHYSICIAN.
It is not strange that a bought watcher drowses;
What is most strange is that the Queen sleeps

KING LEAR'S WIFE

Who would not sleep for all my draughts of sleep
In the last days. When did this change appear?

MERRYN.
We shall not know—it came while Gormflaith
    nodded.
When I awoke her and she saw the Queen
She could not speak for fear:
When the rekindling lamp showed certainly
The bed-clothes stirring about our lady's neck,
She knew there was no death, she breathed, she
    said
She had not slept until her mistress slept
And lulled her; but I asked her how her mistress
Slept, and her utterance faded.
She should be blamed with rods, as I was blamed
For slumber, after a day and a night of watching,
By the Queen's child-bed, twenty years ago.

LEAR.
She does what she must do: let her alone.
I know her watch is now: get gone and send her.
      MERRYN *goes out by the door beyond the*
        bed.
Is it a portent now to sleep at night?
What change is here? What see you in the Queen?
Can you discern how this disease will end?

PHYSICIAN.
Surmise might spring and healing follow yet,
If I could find a trouble that could heal;
But these strong inward pains that keep her ebbing
Have not their source in perishing flesh.
I have seen women creep into their beds
And sink with this blind pain because they nursed

KING LEAR'S WIFE

Some bitterness or burden in the mind
That drew the life, sucklings too long at breast.
Do you know such a cause in this poor lady?

LEAR.
There is no cause. How should there be a cause?

PHYSICIAN.
We cannot die wholly against our wills;
And in the texture of women I have found
Harder determination than in men:
The body grows impatient of enduring,
The harried mind is from the the body estranged,
And we consent to go: by the Queen's touch,
The way she moves—or does not move—in bed,
The eyes so cold and keen in her white mask,
I know she has consented.
The snarling look of a mute wounded hawk,
That would be let alone, is always hers—
Yet she was sorely tender: it may be
Some wound in her affection will not heal.
We should be careful—the mind can so be hurt
That nought can make it be unhurt again.
Where, then, did her affection most persist?

LEAR.
Old bone-patcher, old digger in men's flesh,
Doctors are ever itching to be priests,
Meddling in conduct, natures, life's privacies.
We have been coupled now for twenty years,
And she has never turned from me an hour—
She knows a woman's duty and a queen's:
Whose, then, can her affection be but mine?
How can I hurt her—she is still my queen?
If her strong inward pain is a real pain
Find me some certain drug to medicine it:

9

KING LEAR'S WIFE

When common beings have decayed past help,
There must be still some drug for a king to use;
For nothing ought to be denied to kings.

PHYSICIAN.
For the mere anguish there is such a potion.
The gum of warpy juniper shoots is seethed
With the torn marrow of an adder's spine;
An unflawed emerald is pashed to dust
And mingled there; that broth must cool in
  moonlight.
I have indeed attempted this already,
But the poor emeralds I could extort
From wry-mouthed earls' women had no force.
In two more dawns it will be late for potions. . . .
There are not many emeralds in Britain,
And there is none for vividness and strength
Like the great stone that hangs upon your breast:
If you will waste it for her she shall be holpen.

LEAR, *with rising voice.*
Shatter my emerald? My emerald? My emerald?
A High King of Eire gave it to his daughter
Who mothered generations of us, the kings of
  Britain;
It has a spiritual influence; its heart
Burns when it sees the sun   Shatter my
  emerald!
Only the fungused brain and carious mouth
Of senile things could shape such thought. .
    My emerald!
            HYGD *stirs uneasily in her sleep.*

PHYSICIAN.
Speak lower, low; for your good fame, speak low—
If she should waken thus.

10

LEAR.   There is no wise man
Believes that medicine is in a jewel.
It is enough that you have failed with one.
Seek you a common stone. I'll not do it.
Let her eat heartily: she is spent with fasting.
Let her stand up and walk: she is so still
Her blood can never nourish her. Come away.

PHYSICIAN.
I must not leave her ere the woman comes—
Or will some other woman.

LEAR.   No, no, no, no;
The Queen is not herself; she speaks without
     sense;
Only Merryn and Gormflaith understand.
She is better quiet. Come. . . .
          He urges the PHYSICIAN *roughly away by*
          the shoulder.
                         My emerald!
          He follows the PHYSICIAN *out by the door*
          at the back.
          Queen HYGD *awakes at his last noisy*
          words as he disappears.

HYGD.
I have not slept; I did but close mine eyes
A little while—a little while forgetting. . .
Where are you, Merryn? . . . Ah, it is not
     Merryn. . . .
Bring me the cup of whey, woman; I thirst.
Will you speak to me if I say your name?
Will you not listen, Gormflaith?   Can you
     hear?
I am very thirsty—let me drink.

Ah, wicked woman, why did I speak to you?
I will not be your suppliant again.
Where are you? O, where are you?   Where
    are you?

> *She tries to raise herself to look about the
> room, but sinks back helplessly.*
>
> *The curtains of the door at the back are
> parted, and* GONERIL *appears in
> hunting dress,—her kirtle caught up
> in her girdle, a light spear over her
> shoulder—stands there a moment,
> then enters noiselessly and approaches
> the bed. She is a girl just turning to
> womanhood, proud in her poise, swift
> and cold, an almost gleaming pre-
> sence, a virgin huntress.*

GONERIL.
Mother, were you calling?
Have I awakened you?
They said that you were sleeping.
Why are you left alone, mother, my dear one?

HYGD.
Who are you? No, no, no! Stand farther off!
You pulse and glow; you are too vital; your
    presence hurts
Freshness of hill-swards, wind and trodden ling,
I should have known that Goneril stands here.
It is yet dawn, but you have been afoot
Afar and long: where could you climb so soon?

GONERIL.
Dearest, I am an evil daughter to you:
I never thought of you—O, never once—

KING LEAR'S WIFE

Until I heard a moor-bird cry like you.
I am wicked, rapt in joys of breath and life,
And I must force myself to think of you.
I leave you to caretakers' cold gentleness;
But O, I did not think that they dare leave you.
What woman should be here?

HYGD.   I have forgot. . .
I know not   She will be about some duty.
I do not matter: my time is done . . . nigh
      done
Bought hands can well prepare me for a grave,
And all the generations must serve youth.
My girls shall live untroubled while they may,
And learn happiness once while yet blind men
Have injured not their freedom;
For women are not meant for happiness.
Where have you been, my falcon?

GONERIL.
I dreamt that I was swimming, shoulder up,
And drave the bed-clothes spreading to the floor:
Coldness awoke me; through the waning darkness
I heard far hounds give shivering aëry tongue,
Remote, withdrawing, suddenly faint and near;
I leapt and saw a pack of stretching weasels
Hunt a pale coney in a soundless rush,
Their elfin and thin yelping pierced my heart
As with an unseen beauty long awaited;
Wolf-skin and cloak I buckled over this night-
      gear,
And took my honoured spear from my bed-side
Where none but I may touch its purity,
And sped as lightly down the dewy bank
As any mothy owl that hunts quick mice.

13

KING LEAR'S WIFE

They went crying, crying, but I lost them
Before I stept, with the first tips of light,
On Raven Crag near by the Druid Stones;
So I paused there and, stooping, pressed my hand
Against the stony bed of the clear stream;
Then entered I the circle and raised up
My shining hand in cold stern adoration
Even as the first great gleam went up the sky.

HYGD.
Ay, you do well to worship on that height:
Life is free to the quick up in the wind,
And the wind bares you for a god's descent—
For wind is a spirit immediate and aged.
And you do well to worship harsh men-gods,
God Wind and Those who built his Stones with
          him:
All gods are cruel, bitter, and to be bribed,
But women-gods are mean and cunning as well.
That fierce old virgin, Cornish Merryn, prays
To a young woman, yes and even a virgin—
The poorest kind of woman—and she says
That is to be a Christian: avoid then
Her worship most, for men hate such denials,
And any woman scorns her unwed daughter.
Where sped you from that height? Did Regan
          join you there?

GONERIL.
Does Regan worship anywhere at dawn?
The sweaty half-clad cook-maids render lard
Out in the scullery, after pig-killing,
And Regan sidles among their greasy skirts,
Smeary and hot as they, for craps to suck.
I lost my thoughts before the giant Stones . .

14

And when anew the earth assembled round me
I swung out on the heath and woke a hare
And speared it at a cast and shouldered it,
Startled another drinking at a tarn
And speared it ere it leapt; so steady and clear
Had the god in his fastness made my mind.
Then, as I took those dead things in my hands,
I felt shame light my face from deep within,
And loathing and contempt shake in my bowels,
That such unclean coarse blows from me had
     issued
To crush delicate things to bloody mash
And blemish their fur when I would only kill.
My gladness left me; I careered no more
Upon the morning; I went down from there
With empty hands:
But under the first trees and without thought
I stole on conies at play and stooped at one;
I hunted it, I caught it up to me
As I outsprang it, and with this thin knife
Pierced it from eye to eye; and it was dead,
Untorn, unsullied, and with flawless fur.
Then my untroubled mind came back to me.

HYGD.
Leap down the glades with a fawn's ignorance;
Live you your fill of a harsh purity;
Be wild and calm and lonely while you may.
These are your nature's joys, and it is human
Only to recognize our natures' joys
When we are losing them for ever.

GONERIL.   But why
Do you say this to me with a sore heart?
You are a queen, and speak from the top of life,

And when you choose to wish for others' joys
Those others must have woe.

HYGD.
The hour comes for you to turn to a man
And give yourself with the high heart of youth
More lavishly than a queen gives anything.
But when a woman gives herself
She must give herself for ever and have faith;
For woman is a thing of a season of years,
She is an early fruit that will not keep,
She can be drained and as a husk survive
To hope for reverence for what has been;
While man renews himself into old age,
And gives himself according to his need,
And women more unborn than his next child
May take him yet with youth
And lose him with their potence.

GONERIL.
But women need not wed these men.

HYGD.
We are good human currency, like gold,
For men to pass among them when they choose.
A child's hands beat on the outside of the
door beyond the bed.

CORDEIL'S VOICE, *a child's voice, outside.*
Father.   Father   Father. . . . Are you
    here?
Merryn, ugly Merryn, let me in. . . .
I know my father is here. . . . I want him. . .
    Now. . . .
Mother, chide Merryn, she is old and slow. . . .

HYGD, *softly*.
My little curse. Send her away—away. . . .

CORDEIL'S VOICE.
Father.   O, father, father.   I want my
    father.

GONERIL, *opening the door a little way*.
Hush; hush—you hurt your mother with your
    voice.
You cannot come in, Cordeil; you must go away:
Your father is not here. . . .

CORDEIL'S VOICE.   He must be here:
He is not in his chamber or the hall,
He is not in the stable or with Gormflaith·
He promised I should ride with him at dawn
And sit before his saddle and hold his hawk,
And ride with him and ride to the heron-marsh;
He said that he would give me the first heron,
And hang the longest feathers in my hair.

GONERIL.
Then you must haste to find him;
He may be riding now.

CORDEIL'S VOICE.
But Gerda said she saw him enter here.

GONERIL.
Indeed, he is not here. . . .

CORDEIL'S VOICE.   Let me look. ..

GONERIL.
You are too noisy. Must I make you go?

CORDEIL'S VOICE.
Mother, Goneril is unkind to me.

HYGD, *raising herself in bed excitedly, and speaking so vehemently that her utterance strangles itself.*
Go, go, thou evil child, thou ill-comer.
> GONERIL, *with a sudden strong movement, shuts the resisting door and holds it rigidly. The little hands beat on it madly for a moment, then the child's voice is heard in a retreating wail.*

GONERIL.
Though she is wilful, obeying only the King,
She is a very little child, mother,
To be so bitterly thought of.

HYGD.
Because a woman gives herself for ever
Cordeil the useless had to be conceived
(Like an after-thought that deceives nobody)
To keep her father from another woman.
And I lie here.

GONERIL, *after a silence.*
Hard and unjust my father has been to me;
Yet that has knitted up within my mind
A love of coldness and a love of him
Who makes me firm, wary, swift and secret,
Until I feel if I become a mother
I shall at need be cruel to my children,
And ever cold, to string their natures harder
And make them able to endure men's deeds;
But now I wonder if injustice

Keeps house with baseness, taught by kinship—
I never thought a king could be untrue,
I never thought my father was unclean
O mother, mother, what is it? Is this dying?

HYGD.
I think I am only faint. . . .
Give me the cup of whey. . .
>   GONERIL *takes the cup and, supporting*
>   HYGD, *lets her drink.*

GONERIL.
There is too little here. When was it made?

HYGD.
Yester-eve. . . . Yester-morn. . . .

GONERIL.   Unhappy mother,
You have no daughter to take thought for you—
No servant's love to shame a daughter with,
Though I am shamed—you must have other food,
Straightway I bring you meat. . . .

HYGD.   It is no use. . . .
Plenish the cup for me. . . . Not now, not now,
But in a while; for I am heavy now. . . .
Old Wynoc's potions loiter in my veins,
And tides of heaviness pour over me
Each time I wake and think. I could sleep now.

GONERIL.
Then I shall lull you, as you once lulled me.
>   *Seating herself on the bed, she sings.*
>   The owlets in roof-holes
>   Can sing for themselves;
>   The smallest brown squirrel
>   Both scampers and delves;

But a baby does nothing—
She never knows how—
She must hark to her mother
Who sings to her now.
Sleep then, ladykin, peeping so;
Hide your handies and ley lei lo.

> *She bends over* HYGD *and kisses her; they laugh softly together.*
>
> LEAR *parts the curtains of the door at the back, stands there a moment, then goes away noiselessly.*

The lish baby otter
Is sleeky and streaming,
With catching bright fishes,
Ere babies learn dreaming;
But no wet little otter
Is ever so warm
As the fleecy-wrapt baby
'Twixt me and my arm.
Sleep big mousie. . . .

HYGD, *suddenly irritable.*

> Be quiet. . . . I cannot bear it.
>
> *She turns her head away from* GONERIL *and closes her eyes.*
>
> *As* GONERIL *watches her in silence,* GORMFLAITH *enters by the door beyond the bed. She is young and tall and fresh-coloured; her red hair coils and crisps close to her little head, showing its shape. Her movements are soft and unhurried; her manner is quiet and ingratiating and a little too agreeable; she speaks a little too gently.*

GONERIL, *meeting her near the door and speaking
in a low voice.*
Why did you leave the Queen? Where have you
been?
Why have you so neglected this grave duty?

GORMFLAITH.
This is the instant of my duty, Princess:
From midnight until now was Merryn's watch.
I thought to find her here: is she not here?
> HYGD *turns to look at the speakers; then,
turning back, closes her eyes again
and lies as if asleep.*

GONERIL.
I found the Queen alone. I heard her cry your
name.

GORMFLAITH.
Your anger is not too great, Madam; I grieve
That one so old as Merryn should act thus—
So old and trusted and favoured, and so callous.

GONERIL.
The Queen has had no food since yester-night.

GORMFLAITH.
Madam, that is too monstrous to conceive:
I will seek food—I will prepare it now.

GONERIL.
Stay here: and know, if the Queen is left again,
You shall be beaten with two rods at once.
> *She picks up the cup and goes out by the
door beyond the bed.*

KING LEAR'S WIFE

GORMFLAITH *turns the chair a little away from the bed so that she can watch the far door, and, seating herself, draws a letter from her bosom.*

GORMFLAITH, *to herself, reading.*
"Open your window when the moon is dead,
And I will come again.
The men say everywhere that you are faithless,
The women say your face is a false face
And your eyes shifty eyes. Ah, but I love you,
    Gormflaith.
Do not forget your window-latch to-night,
For when the moon is dead the house is still."

LEAR *again parts the door-curtains at the back, and, seeing* GORMFLAITH, *enters. At the first slight rustle of the curtains* GORMFLAITH *stealthily slips the letter back into her bosom before turning gradually, a finger to her lips, to see who approaches her.*

LEAR, *leaning over the side of her chair.*
Lady, what do you read?

GORMFLAITH.   I read a letter, Sire.

LEAR.
A letter—a letter—what read you in a letter?

GORMFLAITH, *taking another letter from her girdle.*
Your words to me—my lonely joy your words. . . .
"If you are steady and true as your gaze"—

22

LEAR, *tearing the letter from her, crimpling it, and flinging it to the back of the room.*

Pest!
You should not carry a king's letters about,
Nor hoard a king's letters.

GORMFLAITH.   No, Sire.

LEAR.
Must the King also stand in the presence now?

GORMFLAITH, *rising.*
Pardon my troubled mind; you have taken my
  letter from me.

*LEAR seats himself and takes GORM-
FLAITH'S hand.*

GORMFLAITH.
Wait, wait—I might be seen. The Queen may
  waken yet.

*Stepping lightly to the bed, she noiselessly
slips the curtain on that side as far
forward as it will come. Then she
returns to LEAR, who draws her to
him and seats her on his knee.*

LEAR.
You have been long in coming:
Was Merryn long in finding you?

GORMFLAITH, *playing with LEAR'S emerald.*

Did Merryn. . . .
Has Merryn been. . . . She loitered long before
  she came,
For I was at the women's bathing-place ere
  dawn. . . .

No jewel in all the land excites me and enthralls
Like this strong source of light that lives upon
    your breast.

LEAR, *taking the jewel-chain from his neck and*
    slipping it over GORMFLAITH'S *head while she*
    still holds the emerald.
Wear it within your breast to fill the gentle place
That cherished the poor letter lately torn from you.

GORMFLAITH.
Did Merryn at your bidding, then, forsake her
    Queen?
                            LEAR *nods.*
You must not, ah, you must not do these master-
    ful things,
Even to grasp a precious meeting for us two;
For the reproach and chiding are so hard to me,
And even you can never fight the silent women
In hidden league against me, all this house of
    women.
Merryn has left her Queen in unwatched lone-
    liness,
And yet your daughter Princess Goneril has said
(With lips that scarce held back the spittle for my
    face)
That if the Queen is left again I shall be whipt.

LEAR.
Children speak of the punishments they know.
Her back is now not half so white as yours,
And you shall write your will upon it yet.

GORMFLAITH.
Ah, no, my King, my faithful. . Ah, no. . no . .

24

KING LEAR'S WIFE

The Princess Goneril is right; she judges me:
A sinful woman cannot steadily gaze reply
To the cool, baffling looks of virgin untried force.
She stands beside that crumbling mother in her
    hate,
And, though we know so well—she and I, O we
    know—
That she could love no mother nor partake in
    anguish,
Yet she is flouted when the King forsakes her
    dam,
She must protect her very flesh, her tenderer flesh,
Although she cannot wince; she's wild in her cold
    brain,
And soon I must be made to pay a cruel price
For this one gloomy joy in my uncherished life.
Envy and greed are watching me aloof
(Yes, now none of the women will walk with me),
Longing to see me ruined, but she'll do it.
It is a lonely thing to love a king. . . .

> *She puts her cheek gradually closer and*
> *closer to* LEAR's *cheek as she speaks:*
> *at length he kisses her suddenly and*
> *vehemently, as if he would grasp her*
> *lips with his: she receives it passively,*
> *her head thrown back, her eyes closed.*

LEAR.
Goldilocks, when the crown is couching in your
    hair
And those two mingled golds brighten each
    other's wonder,
You shall produce a son from flesh unused—
Virgin I chose you for that, first crops are
    strongest—
A tawny fox with your high-stepping action,

25

With your untiring power and glittering eyes,
To hold my lands together when I am done,
To keep my lands from crumbling into mouthfuls
For the short jaws of my three mewling vixens.
Hatch for me such a youngster from my seed,
And I and he shall rein my hot-breathed wenches
To let you grind the edges off their teeth.

GORMFLAITH, *shaking her head sadly*.
Life holds no more than this for me; this is my
    hour.
When she is dead I know you'll buy another
    Queen
Giving a county for her, gaining a duchy with
    her—
And put me to wet nursing, leashing me with the
    thralls.
It will not be unbearable—I've had your love.
Master and friend, grant then this hour to me:
Never again, maybe, can we two sit
At love together, unwatched, unknown of all,
In the Queen's chamber, near the Queen's crown
And with no conscious Queen to hold it from us:
Now let me wear the Queen's true crown on me
And snatch a breathless knowledge of the feeling
Of what it would have been to sit by you
Always and closely, equal and exalted,
To be my light when life is dark again.

LEAR.
Girl, by the black stone god, I did not think
You had the nature of a chambermaid,
Who pries and fumbles in her lady's clothes
With her red hands, or on her soily neck
Stealthily hangs her lady's jewels or pearls.
You shall be tiring-maid to the next queen

And try her crown on every day o' your life
In secrecy, if that is your desire:
If you would be a queen, cleanse yourself quickly
Of menial fingering and servile thought.

GORMFLAITH.
You need not crown me. Let me put it on
As briefly as a gleam of Winter sun.
I will not even warm it with my hair.

LEAR.
You cannot have the nature of a queen
If you believe that there are things above you:
Crowns make no queens, queens are the cause of
    crowns.

GORMFLAITH, *slipping from his knee.*
Then I will take one. Look.
        She tip-toes lightly round the front of the
        bed to where the crown hangs on the
        wall.

LEAR.
Come here, mad thing—come back!
Your shadow will wake the Queen.

GORMFLAITH.
Hush, hush! That angry voice
Will surely wake the Queen.
        She lifts the crown from the peg, and re-
        turns with it.

LEAR.
Go back; bear back the crown:
Hang up the crown again.
We are not helpless serfs
To think things are forbidden
And steal them for our joy.

GORMFLAITH.
Hush! Hush! It is too late;
I dare not go again.

LEAR.
Put down the crown: your hands are base hands
    yet.
Give it to me: it issues from my hands.

GORMFLAITH, *seating herself on his knee again,*
    and crowning herself
Let anger keep your eyes steady and bright
To be my guiding mirror: do not move.
You have received two queens within your eyes.
        She laughs clearly, like a bird's sudden
        song. HYGD *awakes and, after an in-*
        stant's bewilderment, turns her head
        toward the sound; finding the bed-
        curtain dropt, she moves it aside a
        little with her fingers; she watches
        LEAR *and* GORMFLAITH *for a short*
        time, then the curtain slips from her
        weak grasp and she lies motionless.

LEAR, *continuing meanwhile.*
Doff it. (GORMFLAITH *hisses him.*) Enough. (*Kiss*)
    Unless you do (*Kiss*) my will (*Kiss*)
I shall (*Kiss*) I shall (*Kiss*) I'll have you (*Kiss*)
    sent (*Kiss*) to (*Kiss*)——

GORMFLAITH.   Hush.

LEAR.
Come to the garden: you shall hear me there.

KING LEAR'S WIFE

GORMFLAITH.
I dare not leave the Queen. . . . Yes, yes, I come.

LEAR.
No, you are better here: the guard would see you.

GORMFLAITH.
Not when we reach the pathway near the apple-
yard. *They rise.*

LEAR.
Girl, you are changed: you yield more beauty so.
> *They go out hand in hand by the door-
> way at the back. As they pass the
> crumpled letter* GORMFLAITH *drops
> her handkerchief on it, then picks up
> handkerchief and letter together and
> thrusts them into her bosom as she
> passes out.*

HYGD, *fingering back the bed-curtain again.*
How have they vanished? What are they doing
now?

GORMFLAITH, *outside, singing to a quick, chatter-
ing tune.*
If you have a mind to kiss me
You shall kiss me in the dark:
Yet rehearse, or you might miss me—
Make my mouth your noontide mark. .
> GORMFLAITH'S *voice grows fainter as the
> song progresses, until all sound is
> lost.*

HYGD.
Does he remember love-ways used with me?

29

KING LEAR'S WIFE

Shall I never know? Is it too near?
I'll watch him at his wooing once again,
Though I peer up at him across my grave-sill.
> *She gets out of bed and takes several steps
> toward the garden doorway; she tot
> ters and sways, then, turning, stum-
> bles back to the bed for support.*

Limbs, will you die? It is not yet the time.
I know more discipline: I'll make you go.
> *She fumbles along the bed to the head,
> then, clinging against the wall,
> drags herself toward the back of the
> room.*

It is too far. I cannot see the wall.
I will go ten more steps: only ten more.
One. Two. Three. Four. Five.
Six. Seven. Eight. Nine. Ten.
Sundown is soon to-day: it is cold and dark.
Now ten steps more, and much will have been
    done.
One. Two. Three. Four. Ten.
Eleven. Twelve. Sixteen. Nineteen. Twenty.
Twenty-one.   Twenty-three.   Twenty-eight.
    Thirty. Thirty-one.
At last the turn. Thirty-six. Thirty-nine. Forty.
Now only once again. Two. Three.
What do the voices say? I hear too many.
The door: but here there is no garden. . . . Ah!
> *She holds herself up an instant by the
> door-curtains; then she reels and falls,
> her body in the room, her head and
> shoulders beyond the curtains.*
> GONERIL *enters by the door beyond the
> bed, carrying the filled cup carefully
> in both hands.*

KING LEAR'S WIFE

GONERIL.
Where are you? What have you done? Speak to
me.

> *Turning and seeing* HYGD, *she lets the
> cup fall and leaps to the open door by
> the bed.*

Merryn, hither, hither.   Mother, O mother!

> *She goes to* HYGD. MERRYN *enters.*

MERRYN.
Princess, what has she done? Who has left her?
She must have been alone.

GONERIL.   Where is Gormflaith?

MERRYN.
Mercy o' mercies, everybody asks me
For Gormflaith, then for Gormflaith, then for
      Gormflaith,
And I ask everybody else for her;
But she is nowhere, and the King will foam.
Send me no more; I am old with running about
After a bodiless name.

GONERIL.   She has been here,
And she has left the Queen. This is her deed.

MERRYN.
Ah, cruel, cruel! The shame, the pity—

GONERIL.   Lift.

> *Together they raise* HYGD, *and carry her
> to bed.*

She breathes, but something flitters under her
      flesh:
Wynoc the leech must help us now. Go, run,

31

Seek him, and come back quickly, and do not
    dare
To come without him.

MERRYN.   It is useless, lady:
There 's fever at the cowherd's in the marsh,
And Wynoc broods above it twice a day,
And I have lately seen him hobble thither.

GONERIL.
I never heard such scornful wickedness
As that a king's physician so should choose
To watch and even heal base men and poor—
And, more than all, when there 's a queen a-
    dying. . . .

HYGD, *recovering conscousness.*
Whence come you, dearest daughter? What have
    I done?
Are you a dream? I thought I was alone.
Have you been hunting on the Windy Height?
Your hands are not thus gentle after hunting.
Or have I heard you singing through my sleep?
Stay with me now: I have had piercing thoughts
Of what the ways of life will do to you
To mould and maim you, and I have a power
To bring these to expression that I knew not.
Why do you wear my crown? Why do you wear
My crown I say? Why do you wear my crown?
I am falling, falling! Lift me: hold me up.
        GONERIL *clmbs on the bed and sυpports*
          HYGD *agaınst her shoυlder.*
It is the bed that breaks, for still I sink.
Grip harder: I am slipping!

KING LEAR'S WIFE

GONERIL.   Woman, help!
> MERRYN *hurries round to the front of the bed and supports* HYGD *on her other side.*
> HYGD *points at the far corner of the room.*

HYGD.
Why is the King's mother standing there?
She should not wear her crown before me now.
Send her away, she had a savage mind.
Will you not hang a shawl across the corner
So that she cannot stare at me again?
> *With a rending sob she buries her face in* GONERIL'S *bosom.*
Ah, she is coming! Do not let her touch me!
Brave splendid daughter, how easily you save me:
But soon will Gormflaith come, she stays for ever.
O, will she bring my crown to me once more?
Yes, Gormflaith, yes. . . .   Daughter, pay Gorm-
flaith well.

GONERIL.
Gormflaith has left you lonely:
'Tis Gormflaith who shall pay.

HYGD.
No, Gormflaith; Gormflaith. . . . Not my loneli-
ness
Everything. . . . Pay Gormflaith. . . .
> *Her head falls back over* GONERIL'S *shoulder and she dies.*

GONERIL, *laying* HYGD *down in bed again.*
Send horsemen to the marshes for the leech

KING LEAR'S WIFE

And let them bind him on a horse's back
And bring him swiftlier than an old man rides.

MERRYN.
This is no leech's work: she's a dead woman.
I'd best be finding if the wisdom-women
Have come from Brita's child-bed to their drinking
By the cook's fire, for soon she'll be past handling.

GONERIL.
This is not death: death could not be like this.
She is quite warm—though nothing moves in her.
I did not know death could come all at once:
If life is so ill-seated no one is safe.
Cannot we leave her like herself awhile?
Wait awhile, Merryn. . . . No, no, no; not yet!

MERRYN.
Child, she is gone and will not come again
However we cover our faces and pretend
She will be there if we uncover them.
I must be hasty, or she'll be as stiff
As a straw mattress is.
            She hurries out by the door near the bed.

GONERIL, *throwing the whole length of her body
      along* HYGD'S *body, and embracing it.*
Come back, come back; the things I have not
      done
Beat in upon my brain from every side:
I know not where to put myself to bear them:
If I could have you now I could act well.
My inward life, deeds that you have not known,
I burn to tell you in a sudden dread
That now your ghost discovers them in me.

34

Hearken, mother; between us there's a bond
Of flesh and essence closer than love can cause:
It cannot be unknit so soon as this,
And you must know my touch,
And you shall yield a sign.
Feel, feel this urging throb: I call to you. Come
    back.
        GORMFLAITH, *still crowned, enters by the*
        garden doorway.

GORMFLAITH.
Come back! Help me and shield me!
        She disappears through the curtains.
        GONERIL *has sprung to her feet at the first*
        sound of GORMFLAITH'S *voice.*
        LEAR *enters by the garden doorway, lead-*
        ing GORMFLAITH *by the hand.*

LEAR.   What is to do?

GONERIL, *advancing to meet them with a deep*
    obeisance.
O, Sir, the Queen is dead: long live the Queen.
You have been ready with the coronation.

LEAR.
What do you mean? Young madam, will you
    mock?

GONERIL.
But is not she your choice?
The old Queen thought so, for I found her here,
Lipping the prints of her supplanter's feet,
Prostrate in homage, on her face, silent.
I tremble within to have seen her fallen down.
I must be pardoned if I scorn your ways:

You cannot know this feeling that I know,
You are not of her kin or house; but I
Share blood with her, and, though she grew too
    worn
To be your Queen, she was my mother, Sir.

GORMFLAITH.
The Queen has seen me.

LEAR.   She is safe in bed.

GONERIL.
Do not speak low: your voice sounds guilty so;
And there is no more need—she will not wake.

LEAR.
She cannot sleep for ever. When she wakes
I will announce my purpose in the need
Of Britain for a prince to follow me,
And tell her that she is to be deposed.
What have you done? She is not breathing now.
She breathed here lately. Is she truly dead?

GONERIL.
Your graceful consort steals from us too soon:
Will you not tell her that she should remain—
If she can trust the faith you keep with a queen?
        She steps to GORMFLAITH, *who is sidling*
           toward the garden doorway, and,
           taking her hand, leads her to the foot
           of the bed.
Lady, why will you go? The King intends
That you shall soon be royal, and thereby
Admitted to our breed: then stay with us
In this domestic privacy to mourn

The grief here fallen on our family.
Kneel now; I yield the eldest daughter's place.
Why do you fumble in your bosom so?
Put your cold hands together; close your eyes,
In inward isolation to assemble
Your memories of the dead, your prayers for her.

> *She turns to* LEAR, *who has approached*
> *the bed and drawn back the curtain.*

What utterance of doom would the king use
Upon a watchman in the castle garth
Who left his gate and let an enemy in?
The watcher by the Queen thus left her station:
The sick bruised Queen is dead of that neglect.
And what should be the doom on a seducer
Who drew that sentinel from his fixt watch?

LEAR.
She had long been dying, and she would have died
Had all her dutiful daughters tended her bed.

GONERIL.
Yes, she had long been dying in her heart.
She lived to see you give her crown away;
She died to see you fondle a menial:
These blows you dealt now, but what elder wounds
Received them to such purpose suddenly?
What had you caused her to remember most?
What things would she be like to babble over
In the wild helpless hour when fitful life
No more can choose what thoughts it shall en-
    courage
In the tost mind? She has suffered you twice over,
Your animal thoughts and hungry powers, this
    day,
Until I knew you unkingly and untrue.

37

KING LEAR'S WIFE

LEAR.
Punishment once taught you daughterly silence;
It shall be tried again. . . . What has she said?

GONERIL.
You cannot touch me now I know your nature:
Your force upon my mind was only terrible
When I believed you a cruel flawless man.
Ruler of lands and dreaded judge of men,
Now you have done a murder with your mind
Can you see any murderer put to death?
Can you

LEAR.   What has she said?

GONERIL.
Continue in your joy of punishing evil,
Your passion of just revenge upon wrong-doers,
Unkingly and untrue?

LEAR.   Enough: what do you know?

GONERIL.
That which could add a further agony
To the last agony, the daily poison
Of her late, withering life; but never word
Of fairer hours or any lost delight.
Have you no memory, either, of her youth,
While she was still to use, spoil, forsake,
That maims your new contentment with a longing
For what is gone and will not come again?

LEAR.
I did not know that she could die to-day.
She had a bloodless beauty that cheated me:
She was not born for wedlock. She shut me out.

She is no colder now. . . . I'll hear no more.
You shall be answered afterward for this.
Put something over her: get her buried:
I will not look on her again.

> *He breaks from* GONERIL *and flings
> abruptly out by the door near the bed.*

GORMFLAITH.
My King, you leave me!

GONERIL.   Soon we follow him:
But, ah, poor fragile beauty, you cannot rise
While this grave burden weights your drooping
    head.

> *Laying her hand caressingly on* GORM-
> FLAITH'S *neck, she gradually forces
> her head farther and farther down.*

You were not nurtured to sustain a crown,
Your unanointed parents could not breed
The spirit that ten hundred years must ripen.
Lo, how you sink and fail.

GORMFLAITH.   You had best take care,
For where my neck has bruises yours shall have
    wounds.
The King knows of your wolfish snapping at me:
He will protect me.

GONERIL.   Ay, if he is in time.

GORMFLAITH, *taking off the crown and holding it
up blindly toward* GONERIL *with one hand.*
Take it and let me go!

GONERIL.   Nay, not to me:
You are the Queen's, to serve her even in death.

Yield her her own. Approach her: do not fear;
She will not chide you or forgive you now.
Go on your knees; the crown still holds you down.

> GORMFLAITH *stumbles forward on her*
> *knees and lays the crown on the bed,*
> *then crouches motionlessly against the*
> *bedside.*

GONERIL, *taking the crown and putting it on the*
> *dead Queen's head.*

Mother and Queen, to you this holiest circlet
Returns, by you renews its purpose and pride;
Though it is sullied with a menial warmth,
Your august coldness shall rehallow it,
And when the young lewd blood that lent it heat
Is also cooler we can well forget.

> *She steps to* GORMFLAITH.

Rise. Come, for here there is no more to do,
And let us seek your chamber, if you will,
There to confer in greater privacy;
For we have now interment to prepare.

> *She leads* GORMFLAITH *to the door near*
> *the bed.*

You must walk first, you are still the Queen elect.

> *When* GORMFLAITH *has passed before her*
> GONERIL *unsheathes her hunting*
> *knife.*

GORMFLAITH, *turning in the doorway.*
What will you do?

GONERIL, *thrusting her forward with the haft of*
> *the knife.* On. On. On. Go in.

> *She follows* GORMFLAITH *out.*
> *After a moment's interval two elderly*

women, one a little younger than the other, enter by the same door: they wear black hoods and shapeless black gowns with large sleeves that flap like the wings of ungainly birds: between them they carry a heavy cauldron of hot water.

THE YOUNGER WOMAN.
We were listening. We were listening.

THE ELDER WOMAN.   We were both listening.

THE YOUNGER WOMAN.
Did she struggle?

THE ELDER WOMAN.
                She could not struggle long.
They set down the cauldron at the foot of the bed.

THE ELDER WOMAN, *curtseying to the Queen's body.*
Saving your presence, Madam, we are come
To make you sweeter than you'll be hereafter,
And then be done with you.

THE YOUNGER WOMAN, *curtseying in turn.*
Three days together, my Lady, y'have had me ducked
For easing a foolish maid at the wrong time;
But now your breath is stopped and you are colder,
And you shall be as wet as a drowned cat
Ere I have done with you.

41

KING LEAR'S WIFE

THE ELDER WOMAN, *fumbling in the folds of the robe that hangs on the wall.*
Her pocket is empty; Merryn has been here first.
Hearken, and then begin:
You have not touched a royal corpse before,
But I have stretched a king and an old queen,
A king's aunt and a king's brother too,
Without much boasting of a still-born princess;
So that I know, as a priest knows his prayers,
All that is written in the chamberlain's book
About the handling of exalted corpses,
Stripping them and trussing them for the grave:
And there it says that the chief corpse-washer
Shall take for her own use by sacred right
The coverlid, the upper sheet, the mattress
Of any bed in which a queen has died,
And the last robe of state the body wore;
While humbler helpers may divide among them
The under sheet, the pillow, and the bed-gown
Stript from the cooling queen.
Be thankful, then, and praise me every day
That I have brought no other women with me
To spoil you of your share.

THE YOUNGER WOMAN.
Ah, you have always been a friend to me:
Many's the time I have said I did not know
How I could even have lived but for your kindness.
> *The* ELDER WOMAN *draws down the bed-clothes from the Queen's body, loosens them from the bed, and throws them on the floor.*

THE ELDER WOMAN.
Pull her feet straight: is your mind wandering?

42

KING LEAR'S WIFE

She commences to fold the bedclothes,
singing as she moves about.
A louse crept out of my lady's shift—
Ahumm, Ahumm, Ahee—
Crying " Oi! Oi! We are turned adrift;
The lady's bosom is cold and stiffed,
And her arm-pit's cold for me."
While the ELDER WOMAN *sings, the*
YOUNGER WOMAN straightens the
Queen's feet and ties them together,
draws the pillow from under her head,
gathers her hair in one hand and
knots it roughly; then she loosens her
nightgown, revealing a jewel hung on
a cord round the Queen's neck.

THE ELDER WOMAN, *running to the vacant side*
of the bed.
What have you there? Give it to me.

THE YOUNGER WOMAN.   It is mine:
I found it.

THE ELDER WOMAN, *seizing the jewel.*
          Leave it.

THE YOUNGER WOMAN. Let go.

THE ELDER WOMAN.   Leave it, I say.
Will you not? Will you not? An eye for a jewel,
   then!

          She attacks the face of the YOUNGER
          WOMAN *with her disengaged hand.*

THE YOUNGER WOMAN, *starting back.*
          Oh!

43

The ELDER WOMAN *breaks the cord and
  thrusts the jewel into her pocket.*

THE YOUNGER WOMAN.
Aie! Aie! Aie! Old thief! You are always
  thieving!
You stole a necklace on your wedding-day:
You could not bear a child, you stole your
  daughter:
You stole a shroud the morn your husband died:
Last week you stole the Princess Regan's comb . .
> *She stumbles into the chair by the bed, and,
> throwing her loose sleeves over her
> head, rocks herself and moans.*

THE ELDER WOMAN, *resuming her clothes-folding
  and her song.*
  "The lady's linen's no longer neat;"—
Ahumm, Ahumm, Ahee—
  "Her savour is neither warm nor sweet;
It's close for two in a winding-sheet,
And lice are too good for worms to eat;
So here's no place for me."
> GONERIL *enters by the door near the bed:
> her knife and the hand that holds it
> are bloody. She pauses a moment ir-
> resolutely.*

THE ELDER WOMAN.
Still work for old Hrogneda, little Princess?
> GONERIL *goes straight to the cauldron,
> passing the women as if they were not
> there: she kneels and washes her knife
> and her hand in it. The women retire
> to the back of the chamber.*

GONERIL, *speaking to herself*
The way is easy: and it is to be used.
How could this need have been conceived slowly?
In a keen mind it should have leapt and burnt:
What I have done would have been better done
When my sad mother lived and could feel joy.
This striking without thought is better than
    hunting;
She showed more terror than an animal,
She was more shiftless.
A little blood is lightly washed away,
A common stain that need not be remembered;
And a hot spasm of rightness quickly born
Can guide me to kill justly and shall guide.
          LEAR *enters by the door near the bed.*

LEAR.
Goneril, Gormflaith, Gormflaith. . . . Have you
    seen Gormflaith?

GONERIL.
I led her to her chamber lately, Sir.

LEAR.
Ay, she is in her chamber. She is there.

GONERIL.
Have you been there already? Could you not
    wait?

LEAR.
Daughter, she is bleeding: she is slain.

GONERIL, *rising from the cauldron with dripping
    hands.*
Yes, she is slain: I did it with a knife:

45

And in this water is dissolved her blood,
  (*Raising her arms and sprinkling the
    Queen's body*)
That now I scatter on the Queen of death
For signal to her spirit that I can slake
Her long corrosion of misery with such balm—
Blood for weeping, terror for woe, death for death,
A broken body for a broken heart.
What will you say against me and my deed?

LEAR.
That now you cannot save yourself from me.
While your blind virgin power still stood apart
In an unused, unviolated life,
You judged me in my weakness, and because
I felt you unflawed I could not answer you;
But you have mingled in mortality
And violently begun the common life
By fault against your fellows; and the state,
The state of Britain that inheres in me
Not touched by my humanity or sin,
Passions or privy acts, shall be as hard
And savage to you as to a murderess.

GONERIL, *taking a letter from her girdle.*
I found a warrant in her favoured bosom, King:
She wore this on her heart when you were crown-
  ing her.

LEAR, *opening the letter.*
But this is not my hand:
          (*Looking about him on the floor*)
Where is the other letter?

GONERIL.
Is there another letter? What should it say?

K I N G L E A R ' S W I F E

LEAR.
There is no other letter if you have none.
    (*Reading*)
" Open your window when the moon is dead,
And I will come again.
The men say everywhere that you are faithless. . . .
And your eyes shifty eyes. Ah, but I love you,
  Gormflaith. . . ."
This is not hers: she'd not receive such words.

GONERIL.
Her name stands twice therein: her perfume fills it:
My knife went through it ere I found it on her.

LEAR.
The filth is suitably dead. You are my true
  daughter.

GONERIL.
I do not understand how men can govern,
Use craft and exercise the duty of cunning,
Anticipate treason, treachery meet with treachery,
And yet believe a woman because she looks
Straight in their eyes with mournful, trustful
  gaze,
And lisps like innocence, all gentleness.
Your Gormflaith could not answer a woman's
  eyes.
I did not need to read her in a letter;
I am not woman yet, but I can feel
What untruths are instinctive in my kind,
And how some men desire deceit from us.
Come; let these washers do what they must do:
Or shall your Queen be wrapped and coffined
  awry? *She goes out by the garden doorway.*

LEAR.

I thought she had been broken long ago:
She must be wedded and broken, I cannot do it.

> *He follows* GONERIL *out.*
> *The two women return to the bedside.*

THE ELDER WOMAN.

Poor, masterful King, he is no easier,
Although his tearful wife is gone at last:
A wilful girl shall prick and thwart him now.
Old gossip, we must hasten; the Queen is setting.
Lend me a pair of pennies to weight her eyes.

THE YOUNGER WOMAN.

Find your own pennies: then you can steal them
   safely.

THE ELDER WOMAN.

Praise you the gods of Britain, as I do praise
   them,
That I have been sweet-natured from my birth,
And that I lack your unforgiving mind.
Friend of the worms, help me to lift her clear
And draw away the under sheet for you;
Then go and spread the shroud by the hall fire—
I never could put damp linen on a corpse.

> *She sings.*
> The louse made off unhappy and wet;—
> Ahumm, Ahumm, Ahee—
> He's looking for us, the little pet;
> So haste, for her chin's to tie up yet,
> And let us be gone with what we can get—
> Her ring for thee, her gown for Bet,
> Her pocket turned out for me.

CURTAIN.

THE CRIER BY NIGHT

E

TO

MY DEAR SCRIBE

PERSONS:

HIALTI, a Northman.
THORGERD, his Wife.
BLANID, an Irish Bondmaid.
AN OLD STRANGE MAN.

THE CRIER BY NIGHT

The scene is the interior of a cottage near a misty mere and among unseen mountains on a wild night of late Autumn. In the back wall are a door to the left and a long low window in the middle; the latter is shuttered on the outside, and on door and window the wind-driven rain rattles. In the middle of the left-hand wall a door leads into an outhouse; near it is a loom: toward the front of the right-hand wall another door leads to a sleeping-chamber; a settle extends along this wall and in front of it a long table is set. Two rushlights burn on the table. A round hearth is in the middle of the house; its smoke rises into a luffer which hangs from the thatched roof between two beams. The floor is thickly strewn with rushes. There are several wooden stools about the hearth, on one of which HIALTI *is sitting mending harness.* THORGERD *is standing near the loom, spinning with a distaff.*

HIALTI.
THE lass is late about; where is she now?

THORGERD.
Let the lass be. What is the lass to you?

53

THE CRIER BY NIGHT

She is my lass to handle as I will
My father gave her to me for my own,
And so I use her as I use my gear . . .
"She will not last" say you? Well, what of that?
I know gear must wear out, being well used;
Shoes must be trodden under-foot all day,
Though in the mire they go and to the mire;
The hearth-fire wastes the irons used to tend it:
I am the huswife—leave the house to me
And buy me new gear when the old is rotten.

HIALTI.
You drive her over hard. In the cold dark,
Hours ere the thin late dawn, she was afoot,
And she has been afoot each moment since:
The butter will not come now without fire,
But I was wakened in the frosty night
By the slow moaning of her weary churn,
And when I rose she stood here without shoes—
She said you took them from her; so I sought,
And gave her them again, and lit the fire.
She dare not sleep with half your tasks undone,
But you slept and your sleep was all her rest;
Yet in her land 'tis you would be the thrall.
You shut the hens in from the storm all day,
But she must trudge with peat-mull in a swill
Up from the water-side and down all day . . .

THORGERD
Spare her and have my firing spoilt? Not I.
Had it been sodden, how could you light her fires?

HIALTI.
You drive her over hard.

54

THORGERD. What is it to you?
Fodder and yoke your neats, see to your swine,
Put them to breed, and leave my stock to me.
If this is over hard, what will it be—
Last week she still could smile sometimes, so yet
She smiles too often for my happiness.
What money did the calves fetch at the fair?

HIALTI.
Where is she now?

THORGERD. What money did the calves
Fetch at the fair last week?

HIALTI. Where is she now?

THORGERD.
I spilt the water; she must needs draw more.

HIALTI.
The roof-drip at the door would fill her pails.

THORGERD.
What money did the calves fetch at the fair?

HIALTI.
You need not ask; you had it all to hoard.

THORGERD.
You kept some back; who bought them?

HIALTI. He who paid.
*The outside door opens and, as the rain
drives in,* BLANID *enters carrying two
pails of water by a yoke. Her short-*

sleeved, frayed, hempen smock is drip-
ping-wet; an old cart-strap is buckled
about her middle; her ankles are bare,
but her feet are covered by shapeless
brogues; her matted hair is cut short,
and she has an iron collar about her
neck. She sets down her pails, and
with difficulty shuts and bolts the door
against the wind. Then she carries
her pails into the outhouse; as she
moves about within she is heard to
sing to a tired, monotonous tune.

BLANID.

The bird in my heart's a-calling through a far-
fled, tear-grey sea
To the soft slow hills that cherish dim waters
weary for me,
Where the folk of rath and dun trail homeward
silently
In the mist of the early night-fall that drips from
their hair like rain.

The bird in my heart's a-flutter, for the bitter
wind of the sea
Shivers with thyme and woodbine as my body
with memory;
I feel their perfumes ooze in my ears like
melody—
The scent of the mead at the harping I shall
not hear again.

The bird in my heart's a-sinking to a hushed vale
hid in the sea,
Where the moonlit dew o'er dead fighters is
stirred by the feet of the Shee,

THE CRIER BY NIGHT

Who are lovely and old as the earth but younger
    than I can be
Who have known the forgetting of dying to a
    life one lonely pain . . .
                She returns from the outhouse.

THORGERD.
Come here; give me your shoes; quickly, I say.
Why must you go shod softly? Give me your
    shoes.
          She takes them and puts them on the fire.
Is there some joy so deep within you still
That I have missed it though 'tis bright for
    singing?
It shall not be so long; sing while you can.

BLANID.
No joy ever sank deep enough for singing;
Trouble and all the sorrowful ways of men
Must stir the sad unrest that ends in song.
Joy seeks but peace and silence and still thought;
But those who cannot weep must sing for ease,
And in the sound forget the thought that smote it.

THORGERD.
I am made glad, hearing your misery;
Yet all the shapeless, creeping, shivering sounds
You wail about the house will make me share it.
Your songs of faëry and nameless kings
And things that never happened long ago
And an unknown, impossible, shadowy land
Are useless as the starlight after moonset
That will not light men homeward from the fair—
Nay, useless as its melting down thin water:
If you must sing, sing truth to gut-strong tunes—

57

Of Gunnar or of Freya or Andvari,
Vineland the Good and the old Western sea.

BLANID.
Things need not happen that they may be true;
Although impossible, they may be true—
The things that matter happen in the heart.
All earthly truth is true but for a time,
Whilst ages may be altered by one dream—
The things that matter happen in the heart

THORGERD.
Useless as starlight or the aimless wind.

BLANID.
The wind is all the souls of those sad dead
Who will not stay in Heaven for love of earth;
Hither and thither they surge to find the gate
They see and know not on its new, strange side,
For they have learned too much to be let back.
Ah, some have learned too much before they die.
> *As she crosses the horse at the back*
> HIALTI *turns and, catching her hands*
> *in his, draws her toward him.*

HIALTI.
Is it too hard, the thought of that lost vale?

BLANID.
It is too hard, because I must so love it
That were I free I should go there no more,
Lest I should hate it. I must always suffer,
I only suffer this way rather than that—
'Tis the eternal suffering of love
Must search me somehow with love's pitilessness
To make me know all souls; what matter how?

THE CRIER BY NIGHT

O, I am but a troubled dream of God's,
And even His will can alter not His dreams;
Yea, He is dreaming me a little while—
I must be dreamed out to the hardest end,
Returning then to be unknown in Him;
I shall be Him again when He awakes.
Ah, God, awake, and so forget me soon.

THORGERD, *swinging her aside by the collar on
her neck.*
Set on the water for the porridge; go.
   BLANID *goes into the othoise;* THOR-
    GERD *continues to* HIALTI.
Why must you hold her hands and hold her eyes?

HIALTI.
Under each dark grey lash a long tear slid,
Like rain in a wild rose's shadowy curve
Bowed in the wind about the morning twilight.

THORGERD.
Have done; I know; you left the fair at noon
To reach the copse just at the young moon's
  setting—
I could not find her till i' the night-hid copse
A woman's voice sobbed "If he would but
  come "

HIALTI.
It is not true; you know it is not true.
Let her alone; you know that I must love you,
And if she loves me she will know it too
And hurt herself far more than you can hurt her.

THORGERD.
I hear you say it: and afterward? . . . Perhaps
My little shears are sharp as any knife.

HIALTI.
You would not kill her?

THORGERD.   When have I grown kind-hearted?
            *She lays her hand on his shoulder and,
            leaning her mouth to his ear, speaks
            in a low, distinct voice.*
Slit nose and lip and where's her beauty then?
            He starts from his stool.
Nay, are my kinsfolk as far off as hers?
            He turns away as BLANID *enters with an
            iron pot which she hangs from a hook
            over the fire, and a pitcher of milk
            which she sets on the table.*
            THORGERD *takes the pot from the fire.*
Here's too much water; it will never boil
And if it did the mess would be too thin.
            *She pours water from the pot upon the
            floor, then hangs the pot over the fire
            again.*
Set out the bowls, and finger not their lips.
            BLANID *goes again to the outhouse, and,
            returning, sets three bowls with spoons
            on the table, and a jar of meal by the
            hearth.*
Though porridge needs meal you shall not think
      for me;
Do nought until I bid you—once. The grain.
            BLANID *goes yet again to the outhouse
            and returns with a bag of grain.*

60

THE CRIER BY NIGHT

You know what grain is for; why do you stand?
Your feet are mine. Down to the quern. Get down.

BLANID.
There's meal in plenty for to-morrow.

THORGERD, *laying down her distaff to make
    porridge.*   Ay,
But is there meal in plenty for next month?
You may be dead then; therefore you must toil,
That I may need to do no aching tasks
Until my man can buy another drudge
From the next herd; for so we shall forget you.

BLANID, *kneeling by the quern between the window
    and the door, and commencing to grind grain.*
You hate me far too subtly to forget me;
There is not enough kindness in your heart
To let you thus forego your joy of hate.
Then, too, despite the accident of death,
I cannot go from here against my will.

THORGERD.
You shall not die ere I have done with you;
And death shall only come by suffering
Until you are too feeble even to suffer.

BLANID.
The sound of death is ever in mine ears,
Monotonous as the night's infinity
Wherein I was once born where salt winds sweep
The wailing of the waters of the West.
I die, but you can ne'er have done with me.

THORGERD, *the porridge being made.*
Come, drudge, lift off the pot and fill the bowls.

61

THE CRIER BY NIGHT

BLANID, *having filled two bowls.*
The pot is empty.

THORGERD.   But the bowls are full.

HIALTI.
Now give the lass some supper; fill her bowl.

THORGERD, *pouring milk over the porridge.*
There's but enough for two; I'll make no more.
Here, take the pot and scrape it at the quern.
> HIALTI *and* THORGERD *draw stools to the
> table;* BLANID *carries the pot to the
> outhouse and returns to the quern;
> supper proceeds in silence for a few
> moments, then* HIALTI *rises and
> offers his bowl to* BLANID.

HIALTI.
Share with me, lass; I need no more to-night.
> *Before* BLANID *can taste the porridge
> THORGERD strikes the bowl from her
> hand.*

HIALTI, *indignantly, as he reaches to* THORGERD'S
bowl.
She shall have yours; go you and make us
     more
> *He is interrupted by a distant wailing
> which is heard through the storm.*

THE VOICE.
Ohey! Ohey! Ohohey!

BLANID.
Master, I hear one calling in the night.

62

THE CRIER BY NIGHT

HIALTI, *in a subdued voice.*
It is the wind across the chimney-slates.

THE VOICE.
Ohey! Ohohey!

BLANID.
Master, a man is calling in the night.

HIALTI.
An owl, storm-beaten, drowns down the long
    mere.

THE VOICE, *sounding nearer on a gust of wind.*
Ohohey! Ohohey!

BLANID.
Master, one lost is helpless in the night.

THORGERD, *gently and with an eager smile.*
Ay, lass, good lass; go, lass, and seek for him—
Maybe he sinks amid the marshy reeds;
Bring him to warmth and supper and a bed.
I'll shut the door; the light will only daze you.

HIALTI, *leaping to the door in front of* BLANID,
    and setting his back to it.
No, no; back, girl, get back. (*To* THORGERD.)
    You murderess,
You know it is the Crier of the Ford,
Who wakens when the clashing waters rise
And the thick night is choked with level rain.
He is not seen; he was not born; he gathers
His bodiless being from the treacherous tarn.
His aged crying gropes about the storm

THE CRIER BY NIGHT

To snare the spent wayfarer to the ford,
Or draw some pitiful helper to the ford,
And drown them where the unknown water swirls
And strangle them with long brown water-weed:
He seeks their souls for his old soul to feed on,
Because it has no body to nourish it.

THORGERD, *hastily yet sullenly*.
How should I know?
> *She grips* BLANID'S *shoulder and hurries
> her to the outhouse.*
>> Get in with you to your straw.
> *She thrusts her into the outhouse and shuts
> the door upon her; then she turns to*
> HIALTI.
Fool, now I know you love her behind your heart.

HIALTI.
I have no mind to waste a half-spent thrall
To prove I love you; and to buy another
Would need more money than eight red-polled
    stirks.

THORGERD.
Choose between her and me; if you take her,
I take the land.

HIALTI.   I love you overmuch
To set you equally against a thrall.

THORGERD.
What, do I touch you when I touch your fields?

HIALTI.
To-morrow I must drive the sold ewes home
And lead more bedding from the bracken-fell

THE CRIER BY NIGHT

If the storm clears—it is well stacked and dry;
So we must be a-stirring by lantern-light,
Since now you will not have the lass go with me
To milk, but go yourself although three cows
Will not let down their milk to you at all,
You drag their teats so: waking-time comes
    soon
Best get to bed.

THORGERD.
    And leave you to go to your straw's wench?

HIALTI, *taking a rushlight in his hand.*
Here are enough of your unfaithful words;
I'll alter this to-morrow.

THORGERD.   Ay, to-morrow.
    HIALTI *enters the sleeping-chamber; after
    watching the door close upon him,*
    THORGERD, *her hands clenched and
    her arms rigid, swiftly steps half way
    toward the outhouse; then, suddenly
    relaxing into a pause and smiling
    with tight lips as she shakes her head
    slightly and sharply, she turns to the
    table again, doffs her coif and draws
    her hair down, blows out the remain-
    ing rushlight, and follows* HIALTI
    into the sleeping-chamber.
    *Henceforth the cottage is only lit by the
    ever-dying fire. A long, empty silence
    ensues, broken only by the tumult of
    the storm and the tinkle of the sinking
    embers.*

THE CRIER BY NIGHT

Then the outhouse door opens slowly and from it BLANID *steps listeningly across the house, in front of the hearth, to the door of the sleeping-chamber, remaining there for a little time with her ear against the door-boards; then she returns noiselessly across the house, behind the hearth, pausing near the house door.*

BLANID, *in a hushed voice.*
If day were only darkness melting down
From darkness into darkness like this rain,
Lost ere 'tis known, then I might always sleep
And sleep and dream I was a queen once more—
She does not know I was a jewelled queen,
For so I spoil her of new heights of joy
In which she might for haughtiness fondle me.
O, I would sleep in that old Crier's arms,
Enduring silence harder than all else,
A mote shut into one cold, kneaded eyelid
Of the dead mere; and dream into the wind,
And cling to stars lest I should slip through space;
And dream I am the body of him I love,
Who yields me only kindness, never love—
O me, that misery of hopeless kindness.
But I'll not die and leave him to her lips;
Though I can never have him she shall not;
For I can use this body worn to a soul
To barter with that Crier of hidden things
That, if he tangles him in his chill hair,
Then I will follow and follow and follow and
     follow,
Past where the imaged stars ebb past their light
And turn to water under the dark world.

66

THE CRIER BY NIGHT

*She goes out into the storm, leaving the
door open behind her. Presently she
is heard singing to a chant-like, ever-
falling melody.*

I stand in the sick night, whose hid shape is my
    own shape,
  As dazed life in the flickering hearts of old men;
I think like a lean heron with bald head and frayed
    nape
    Motionlessly moulting in a flat pool of a grey
    fen,
    Whose sleep-blinked horny eyes know it can
    ne'er moult again.

My age-long cry droops in the hoar unseen stars
    that shake
    Until their discordant rays make darkness in-
    side the sky;
My bare cry shivers along the slimy rushes of the
    drowned lake—
    Weariful waters, do you hear a soul's hair ting-
    ling your veiled feet nigh?
    I stand outside my keen body, yearning into
    you as I cry

HIALTI, *within.*
Is that the lass sobbing a song in sleep?

THORGERD, *within.*
The wind, the wind, and so as much as she.

BLANID, *still out of doors, singing.*
Old father of many waters, can you feel my soul
    touching yours?
    I know that to greet your calling leaves me no
    more any yea or nay;

THE CRIER BY NIGHT

Yet I too am of kin with lost woods and sedgy
    shores,
    So come secret as your black wind and take the
    dark core of my heart away,
    Ere you beget me on death to be still-born to
    an unlit day.
Ohey! Ohey! Ohohey!

THE VOICE.   Ohohey! Ohey!

HIALTI, *within*.
Is there a woman's voice inside the wind?

THORGERD, *within*.
    the unclean Crier croaking   cover your
    ears
        BLANID *re-enters the house hurriedly;*
        she shuts and bolts the door, hardly
        knowing what she does; she falls on
        her knees with her back to the door,
        breathing quickly and hard, and
        swaying backward and forward, her
        face hid in her hands.
        Again and again a terrible blast of wind
        strains at the unyielding door.

THE VOICE, *close at hand*.
Open, open; I cannot open; open.
I cannot come to you unless you open.

BLANID, *muttering behind her hands*.
I will not go . . . I can do nothing else
It shall not enter . . . O, it is in my heart . . .
      She totters fearfully to the door, after many
      hesitant backward glances, and opens
68

it slowly and as if she had never known how to open it. She reels against the wall and stands there motionlessly, clutching it with flat hands and out-spread arms, as a stooping figure swathed in a rain-coloured, rain-soaked cloak and deep hood enters. Wisps of white hair flitter in the mouth of the hood, and one flicker of the fire-light shows in its depths a soft, shrunken, beardless face with an almost lipless, sunken mouth.

THIS OLD STRANGE MAN, *speaking always in a low, even, mournful voice.*

A spirit calling in an old, old tongue
Forgotten in lost graves in lonesome places;
A spirit huddled in an old, old heart
Like a blind crone crouched o'er a long-dead fire;
A spirit shrinking in the old, old hills,
Dreading to step down water or hollow night:
Some seek me dreaming one last hope of joy;
Some have been made too wise by too much joy
And seek me longing for deeper misery,
Knowing that joy is weary in unending,
Changeless and one and easy in low perfection,
While misery has as many shapes as evil
That all must learn, and is made new for ever
By fear of pain desired for love of passion;
But feel, O you who call me through the night,
I bring you neither joy nor misery
But only rest so slow and sad and sodden
You will not know of it—you shall only rest
And lose your soul in my soul evermore.

69

THE CRIER BY NIGHT

*Sounds of heavy breathing are heard from
the sleeping-chamber during his speak-
ing. He is continually reaching to
BLANID with his muffled, unseen
hands, but she holds them from her as
continually.*

BLANID, *always in an eager, suppressed voice.*
I have known joy—I know not what it was,
Mead-fumes that filled me cooling to one drop;
I have known misery—a self-numbed sting
That showed me but another joy to lose;
These were too small, I will have only rest,
And lose my soul in your soul evermore.
But if I die into your drooping limbs
I must be mingled there with him I love;
You may not reach him by your hoary crying,
But raise some human wail for help and light
And he will come and I must follow him
Past where the imaged moon shakes like a soul
Pausing in death between two unknown worlds.

THE OLD MAN.
A sign, a plighting, and I do your will.

BLANID, *winding her arms about his arms from
one side, so that he cannot touch her, and bury-
ing her face in his hood.*
Kisses. 'Hast drained my soul's blood in each
kiss.

THE OLD MAN.
I go, I go; make me not come again,
For I am in you, you must melt to me
Past where the imaged dark shuts bending lovers'
Close, unseen-imaged faces within life

70

THE CRIER BY NIGHT

Keeping his face turned toward BLANID,
*he recedes to the door, where he ceases
to be seen in the wind that scurries
past.*

THE VOICE, *immediately and far away.*
Help; help; the marsh-lights 'wilder us! A light!
BLANID *shuts the door. The fire has now
sunk so low that as she crosses the
house she is only visible in the half-
dark as a dim shape. She pauses by
the hearth.*

BLANID.
Nay, but I touch toward my joy at last,
And Christ and all His Saints go out like candles
When mass is said and the priest's cup is wiped ...

THE VOICE.
The water laps our waists! Help, help! A light!

BLANID, *running to the sleeping-chamber door.*
Master, I hear a calling
         *After an interval she strikes the door,
         crying loudly.*
                   Master! Master!

HIALTI, *within.*
Has the flood washed into the shippon?

BLANID.   Nay;
There is a pitiful shrieking in the dark.

HIALTI, *within.*
It is the Crier; break sleep no more for that.

THE CRIER BY NIGHT

THORGERD, *within.*
The ox-goad shall reward you when dawn
    comes .
Wake us once more and you shall waken often,
Ay, very often, until you dread to sleep

BLANID.
I heard that trailing cry like maddened fir-boughs;
Now I hear words—is there a woman's wail?

THORGERD, *within.*
A woman? Let her drown.

HIALTI, *within.*   I come. I come.
Reach down the lantern and light it, light it,
    light it.
        Standing on a stool, BLANID *lifts a lantern*
           from a nail in one of the beams and,
           carrying it to the hearth, kneels there
           and seeks to light it with an ember.

THORGERD, *within.*
You shall not go; it is a lie of hers;
You shall not go . . .
        A brief struggle in the sleeping-chamber is
        heard.

HIALTI, *within.*   So; stand you from the door.
Get donned; make up the fire; have water boiling;
And send the wench to lie in your warm form
Ready to cherish what stiffening thing I bring.

BLANID, *to herself, lighting the lantern and smiling*
    mischievously.
Yea, I shall cherish a stiffening thing for her.

72

THE CRIER BY NIGHT

Lantern, you are as dim as a little soul,
Yet the least soul can light a man to Heaven,
And you might lead him home; but I am like
  God,
Who makes souls from His aches—I will not
  ache,
You shall not have a soul, I suck it back.
> *She extinguishes the light.* HIALTI *hurries
> in half-dressed.*

HIALTI.
Canst find a rope?

BLANID, *pointing.*   Behind the settle there.
> *To herself.*
'Tis a good rope and has two rotten strands;
'Twas meant to make good tinder on the morrow.

THE VOICE.
Help; help! A light! Come for the woman's
  sake!

HIALTI, *holding out his hand for the lantern.*
Hearken and haste; give me the lantern—now!

BLANID.
Master, it will not light

HIALTI.   Will the storm pause?

THE VOICE.
Ohohey! Ohohey!

HIALTI.
Will that dark Crier linger? I must go.
73

THE CRIER BY NIGHT

She catches his outstretched hand and kisses it ere, snatching it away, he flings the house door wide open and dashes outside. Soon the sound of his footsteps is lost in the storm.

BLANID *relighting the lantern and starting up.*
Master, Master, the light!
Pausing and sending the lantern crashing on the hearth with both hands.
He shall not have it!
She stands with her hands gripping her breasts, leaning forward toward the open door; her breathlessness is all that is heard; she stretches her arms to the night.

BLANID.
I feel as if my long, long hands could reach
Down to the water's heart to pluck him from it.

THE VOICE.
Will no one ever come?

HIALTI, *out of doors.*   I come; I am nigh.

BLANID.
Ay, he is nigh; but soon he will be far.
I dare not thus fall through the world for him.
O, I shall hear him . do not let me hear him . . .
She throws herself on her face on the floor and, covering her head with the strewn rushes and clasping her hands over them, lies there moaning.

74

THE CRIER BY NIGHT

HIALTI, *far off, shouting ever more madly.*
Thorgerd, Thorgerd . . . your hands   the
     world slips past me . . .
Save . . . under . . . under . . . under
     Aa—h . . .
           The shouting ceases suddenly at its height.

BLANID, *muffled and choking.*
Her name . . her name   why did he not
     think my name? . . .
But she has lost him, and I kissed his hand . . .

THORGERD, *rushing from the sleeping-chamber in*
     her night-gear.
Where is the wench? . . Make haste—another light:
I heard him dying. O, this prater's breath
Will blow his life out   Kindle a light and
     come

THE VOICE.
Ohey! Ohohey! Ohey!

BLANID.
Nay! Nay! Nay! I dare not, I dare not
That Crier will drown me too

THORGERD.   That is nought to me;
Get to your feet   What, shall I seek a way
To supple you?

BLANID.   O, do not hurt me again . . .
He dies . . . it is my deed . . . I dare not come . . .

THORGERD.
You are too mean to stir his life one thought;
It was the Crafty Crier—I heard that wail

THE CRIER BY NIGHT

*The fire is now wholly out, so that the
cottage is absolutely dark and nothing
is visible.*

THE VOICE, *near at hand.*
Ohohey! Ohey!

THORGERD, *fiercely.*
Where are you?   O, the Crier is heaving
   o'er

*A gust of wind and rain is heard to sweep
into the cottage through the open door-
way, shifting the rustling floor-rushes
as though feet touched them.* THE
OLD STRANGE MAN *has entered.*

BLANID, *being heard to start to her feet.*
There is another breathing in the house
He is here . . . this darkness is not black enough,
The darkness at light's core alone could hide me.
Grope for my hand—hold fast and take me
   home . . .
          She is heard to sink to the floor again.

THE OLD STRANGE MAN.
Sister of that old race dead in the hills,
Why will you make me come to you once more?
You know you must go down a long withdrawing
To reach the unlit places of your heart,
Which are the night within my unknown eyes
Beyond all stars; so let me touch you once.
          BLANID *is heard to drag her prostrate body
          through the rushes toward* THORGERD.

BLANID.
Mistress, I am your thrall; you will keep your
   own . . .

THE CRIER BY NIGHT

I clasp your feet, I kiss your clutching feet,
I lick your feet all over with my tongue,
I will tell you somewhat that will yield a vengeance
For you to work; so do not let me go . . .

THE OLD MAN.
I see you, you white terror with shaking flanks,
Straining to feel me with your hard-shut eyes,
But now I need you not; not yet; not yet.
Your man is drowned and this is it who bargained
Its death for his; will you not give it to me?

THORGERD, *laighing*.
I am glad he is dead; now I may only love him,
And know no more that last distress of stooping
So far from me as this at my feet must be.
No vengeancing could pay for thoughts of her:
I will not know that such can be in life,
So I will neither yield nor succour her.
                    She speaks no more, nor moves.

THE OLD MAN.
Give it to me; it is mine, give it to me;
I cannot take it while it touches you.
                    A silence.

BLANID.
I have slain him and I fear to go to him . . .
Put out my eyes, and rope me with the dogs—
Nay, strangle me to-morrow; but save me now.

THE OLD MAN, *his voice growing fainter and
    fainter*.
Ah, come, you daughter of an ancient earth,
Come down among the folk your heart can know,
You darling of the past, you long-dead queen.
Your aged soul is strange among these men,

THE CRIER BY NIGHT

As strange as it would be in Paradise;
But once I knew you ere you were begot,
And in the unchanging silence of my heart
There waits a star for you to finish it.

A silence.

You little trembler of a dew-drop dawn,
You are as old as water that makes new dew;
And when the dew falls it runs down to peace.
The end of sorrow is in sorrow's heart
With those who loved and knew the unknown end
Of mothering you a thousand years ago.
Come, then, from her who shapes new pangs for
     you,
And rest and rest and rest for evermore.

A silence.

One day you will awake and call to me;
And I shall listen for the doubting cry
Until the stars have worn the sky too thin,
And I am drowned within the light beyond . . .

*His voice is lost in the gradual wail of a
     gust of wind; then it is heard outside
     and afar.*

Ohey!

BLANID, *speaking at longer and longer intervals.*
O, you have saved me from such evil things
As writhed like tangled tree-roots outside space
Ere God made Himself from them; and for this
My Virgin shall reach down from God's two knees
Whereon She sits, and kiss you for Her own.
My body was yours; now you have saved my soul
My soul is utterly yours to serve in living,
To clothe your soul and be your very heart
In love and soft, unconscious giving of life.
Mother, I have done evil—punish me;

78

THE CRIER BY NIGHT

Because we loved him, love me and punish me:
I have sinned, I have parted lovers—be cruel to me
And cleanse me that I may keep near you two . . .
Think in how many ways you can torture me;
Let me rake up the fire and heat an iron
For you to have your will upon my body—
One thigh is yet unseared . . . Will you not
    speak? . . .
I love him, I tell you . . . I love him, I love him,
    I love him . . .
I kissed his hand; do you hear? I kissed his
    hand—
Our Hialti's hand . . . I'll make you hurt me yet,
Cold anger is shuddering down your tense thighs;
Feel, this is your foot upon my upturned face,
I lift it across my eyes, wide-open eyes—
Bear down and crush them full of eternal night . . .
Speak to me now . . . O, will you never speak?
You thrust me down into that Crier's bosom;
For in your heart you make me be unborn
Within a lonely place you never heard of,
Yet if I loose your feet he will return
And I must follow and follow and follow and
    follow
Past where my imaged thoughts repeat the world,
Till shattered waters break the imaged dream .
You saved me once; will you undo that great-
    ness? .
We are the tears that God wipes from His eyes:
Lone thoughts will thrust me forth—save me
    from them . . .
Ah, but my lonely love can succour me:
Think, if I drown, 'tis to my Hialti's arms,
To cast you from his heart for ever more;
He will not even know you are forgotten . . .

THE CRIER BY NIGHT

Sister   . Thorgerd . . . . . .
          THORGERD *draws in a long breath so
          sharply that it sounds to stab her re-
          peatedly.*
Ay, you will hate me as you used to do—
Will you not hate me as you used to do?
I was so happy when you still could hate me
I fear it, but you make me go . . . Speak once
          After a long silence BLANID *is heard to
          rise and go slowly to the door.*

BLANID.
Ohey! Ohey!

THE VOICE, *outside.* Ohohey!
          With a laugh of abandonment BLANID *is
          heard to run into the night; there is
          a brief silence; then one far-off, long
          shriek is heard from her.*

THE VOICE.
Ohey! Ohohey!
          In the cottage THORGERD *is heard to fall
          heavily to the floor.*
          *The curtain descends on silence and dark-
          ness.*

THE RIDING TO LITHEND

TO EDWARD THOMAS

HERE in the North we speak of you,
And dream (and wish the dream were true)
That when the evening has grown late
You will appear outside our gate—
As though some Gipsy-Scholar yet
Sought this far place that men forget;
Or some tall hero still unknown,
Out of the Mabinogion,
Were seen at nightfall looking in,
Passing mysteriously to win
His earlier earth, his ancient mind,
Where man was true and life more kind
Lived with the mountains and the trees
And other steadfast presences,
Where large and simple passions gave
The insight and the peace we crave,
And he no more had nigh forgot
The old high battles he had fought.

Ah, pause to-night outside our gate
And enter ere it is too late
To see the garden's deep on deep
And talk a little ere we sleep.

When you were here a year ago
I told you of a glorious woe,
The ancient woe of Gunnar dead
And its proud train of men long sped,
Fit brothers to your noble thoughts;
Then, as their shouts and Gunnar's shouts
Went down once more undyingly
And the fierce saga was put by,
I told you of my old desire
To light again that bygone fire,
To body Hallgerd's ruinous
Great hair and wrangling mouth for us,

82

And hear her voice deny again
That hair to Gunnar in his pain.

Because your heart could understand
The hopes of their primeval land,
The hearts of dim heroic fors
Made clear by tenderness and stors,
You caught my glow and urged me on;
So now the tale is once more done
I turn to you, I bring my play,
Longing, O friend, to hear you say
I have not dwarfed those olden things
Nor tarnisht by my furbishings.

I bring my play, I turn to you
And wish it might to-night be true
That you would seek this old small house
Twixt laurel boughs and apple boughs;
Then I would give it, bravely manned,
To you, and with my play my hand.

30 JUNE 1908.

I. M.

2ND LIEUT. PHILIP EDWARD THOMAS

244th Siege Battery, Royal Garrison Artillery;
killed at a forward observation post in the
battle of Arras, on Easter Monday,
April 9th, 1917.

PERSONS:

GUNNAR HAMUNDSSON.

HALLGERD LONGCOAT, his wife.

RANNVEIG, his mother.

ODDNY, ASTRID, and STEINVOR, Hallgerd's house-women.

ORMILD, a woman thrall.

BIARTEY, JOFRID, and GUDFINN, beggar-women.

GIZUR THE WHITE, MORD VALGARDSSON, THORGRIM THE EASTERLING, THORBRAND THORLEIKSSON and ASBRAND his brother, AUNUND, THORGEIR and HROALD, riders.

Many other Riders and voices of Riders.

In Iceland, A.D. 990.

THE RIDING TO LITHEND

The scene is the hall of Gunnar's house at Lithend in South Iceland. The portion shewn is set on the stage diagonally, so that to the right one end is seen while, from the rear corner of this, one side runs down almost to the left front.

The side wall is low and wainscotted with carved panelling on which hang weapons, shields, and coats of mail. In one place a panel slid aside shews a shut bed.

In front of the panelling are two long benches with a carved high-seat between them. Across the end of the hall are similar panellings and the seats, with corresponding tables, of the women's daïs; behind these and in the gable wall is a high narrow door with a rounded top.

A timber roof slopes down to the side wall and is upheld by cross-beams and two rows of tall pillars which make a rather narrow nave of the centre of the hall. One of these rows runs parallel to the side wall, the pair of pillars before the high-seat being carved and ended with images; of the other row only two pillars are visible at the extreme right.

Within this nave is the space for the hearths, but the only hearth visible is the one near the women's daïs. In the roof above it there is a louvre: the fire glows and no smoke rises. The hall is lit everywhere by the firelight.

85

The rafters over the women's daïs carry a floor at the level of the side walls, forming an open loft which is reached by a wide ladder fixed against the wall: a bed is seen in this loft. Low in the roof at intervals are shuttered casements, one being above the loft: all the shutters are closed.

Near the fire a large shaggy hound is sleeping; and ORMILD, *in the undyed woollen dress of a thrall, is combing wool.*

ODDNY *stands spinning at the far side; near her* ASTRID *and* STEINVOR *sit stitching a robe which hangs between them.*

ASTRID.

NIGHT is a Winter long: and evening falls.
  Night, night and Winter and the heavy snow
Burden our eyes, intrude upon our dreams,
And make of loneliness an earthly place.

ORMILD.

This bragging land of freedom that enthralls me
Is still the fastness of a secret king
Who treads the dark like snow, of old king Sleep.
He works with night, he has stolen death's tool
    frost
That makes the breaking wave forget to fall.

ASTRID.

Best mind thy comb-pot and forget our king
Before the Longcoat helps at thy awaking. . . .
I like not this forsaken quiet house.
The house-men out at harvest in the Isles
Never return. Perhaps they went but now,
Yet I am sore with fearing and expecting

Because they do not come. They will not come.
I like not this forsaken quiet house,
This late last harvest, and night creeping in.

ODDNY.
I like not dwelling in an outlaw's house.
Snow shall be heavier upon some eyes
Than you can tell of—ay, and unseen earth
Shall keep that snow from filling those poor eyes.
This void house is more void by brooding things
That do not happen than by absent men.
Sometimes when I awaken in the night
My throbbing ears are mocking me with rumours
Of crackling beams, beams falling, and loud
    flames.

ASTRID, *pointing to the weapons by the high-seat.*
The bill that Gunnar won in a far sea-fight
Sings inwardly when battle impends; as a harp
Replies to the wind thus answers it to fierceness,
So tense its nature is and the spell of its welding;
Then trust ye well that while the bill is silent
No danger thickens, for Gunnar dies not singly.

STEINVOR.
But women are let forth free when men go burning?

ODDNY.
Fire is a hurrying thing, and fire by night
Can see its way better than men see theirs.

ASTRID.
The land will not be nobler or more holpen
If Gunnar burns and we go forth unsinged.
Why will he break the atonement that was set?
That wise old Njal who has the second sight

THE RIDING TO LITHEND

Foretold his death if he should slay twice over
In the same kin or break the atonement set:
Yet has he done these things and will not care.
Kolskegg, who kept his back in famous fights,
Sailed long ago and far away from us
Because that doom is on him for the slayings;
Yet Gunnar bides although that doom is on him
And he is outlawed by defiance of doom.

STEINVOR.
Gunnar has seen his death: he is spoken for.
He would not sail because, when he rode down
Unto the ship, his horse stumbled and threw him,
His face toward the Lithe and his own fields.
Olaf the Peacock bade him be with him
In his new mighty house so carven and bright,
And leave this house to Rannveig and his sons:
He said that would be well, yet never goes.
Is he not thinking death would ride with him?
Did not Njal offer to send his sons,
Skarphedin ugly and brave and Hauskuld with
    him,
To hold this house with Gunnar, who refused
    them
Saying he would not lead young men to death?
I tell you Gunnar is done. . . . His fetch is out.

ODDNY.
Nay, he's been topmost in so many fights
That he believes he shall fight on untouched.

STEINVOR.
He rides to motes and Things before his foes.
He has sent his sons harvesting in the Isles.
He takes deliberate heed of death—to meet it,

Like those whom Odin needs. He is fey, I tell
    you—
And if we are past the foolish ardour of girls
For heroisms and profitless loftiness
We shall get gone when bedtime clears the house.
'Tis much to have to be a hero's wife,
And I shall wonder if Hallgerd cares about it:
Yet she may kindle to it ere my heart quickens.
I tell you, women, we have no duty here:
Let us get gone to-night while there is time,
And find new harbouring ere the laggard dawn,
For death is making narrowing passages
About this hushed and terrifying house.

> RANNVEIG, *an old wimpled woman, enters
> as if from a door at the inseen end of
> the hall.*

ASTRID.
He is so great and manly, our master Gunnar,
There are not many ready to meet his weapons:
And so there may not be much need of weapons.
He is so noble and clear, so swift and tender,
So much of Iceland's fame in foreign places,
That too many love him, too many honour him
To let him die, lest the most gleaming glory
Of our grey country should be there put out.

RANNVEIG.
My son has enemies, girl, enemies,
Who will not lose the joy of hurting him.
This little land is no more than a lair
That holds too many fiercenesses too straitly,
And no man will refuse the rapture of killing
When outlawry has made it cheap and righteous.
So long as any one perceives he knows

THE RIDING TO LITHEND

A bare place for a weapon on my son
His hand shall twitch to fit a weapon in.
Indeed he shall lose nothing but his life
Because a woman is made so evil fair,
Wasteful and white and proud in harmful acts.
I lose two sons when Gunnar's eyes are still,
For then will Kolskegg never more turn home. . . .
If Gunnar would but sail three years would pass;
Only three years of banishment said the doom—
So few, so few, for I can last ten years
With this unshrunken body and steady heart.
                    (*To* ORMILD)
Have I sat down in comfort by the fire
And waited to be told the thing I knew?
Have any men come home to the young women,
Thinking old women do not need to hear,
That you can play at being a bower-maid
In a long gown although no beasts are foddered?
Up, lass, and get thy coats about thy knees,
For we must cleanse the byre and heap the midden
Before the master knows—or he will go,
And there is peril for him in every darkness.

ORMILD, *ticking up her skirts.*
Then are we out of peril in the darkness?
We should do better to nail up the doors
Each night and all night long and sleep through it,
Giving the cattle meat and straw by day.

ODDNY.
Ay, and the hungry cattle should sing us to sleep.
           The others laugh. ORMILD *goes out to the*
           left; RANNVEIG *is following her, but*
           pauses at the sound of a voice.
                    90

THE RIDING TO LITHEND

HALLGERD, *beyond the door of the women's daïs.*
Dead men have told me I was better than fair,
And for my face welcomed the danger of me:
Then am I spent?
> *She enters angrily, looking backward through the doorway.*

Must I shut fast my doors
And hide myself? Must I wear up the rags
Of mortal perished beauty and be old?
Or is there power left upon my mouth
Like colour, and lilting of ruin in my eyes?
Am I still rare enough to be your mate?
Then why must I shame at feasts and bear myself
In shy ungainly ways, made flushed and conscious
By squat numb gestures of my shapeless head
Ay, and its wagging shadow—clouted up,
Twice tangled with a bundle of hot hair,
Like a thick cot-wife's in the settling time?
There are few women in the Quarter now
Who do not wear a shapely fine-webbed coif
Stitched by dark Irish girls in Athcliath
With golden flies and pearls and glinting things:
Even my daughter lets her big locks show,
Show and half show, from a hood gentle and close
That spans her little head like her husband's hand.

GUNNAR, *entering by the same door.*
I like you when you bear your head so high;
Lift but your heart as high, you could get crowned
And rule a kingdom of impossible things.
You would have moon and sun to shine together,
Snow-flakes to knit for apples on bare boughs,
Yea, love to thrive upon the terms of hate.
If I had fared abroad I should have found
In many countries many marvels for you—

THE RIDING TO LITHEND

Though not more comeliness in peopled Rome-
    borg
And not more haughtiness in Mickligarth
Nor craftiness in all the isles of the world,
And only golden coifs in Athcliath:
Yet you were ardent that I should not sail,
And when I could not sail you laughed out loud
And kissed me home.

HALLGERD, *who has been biting her nails.*
And then . . . and doubtless . . . and strangely . . .
And not more thriftiness in Bergthorsknoll
Where Njal saves old soft sackcloth for his wife.
O, I must sit with peasants and aged women,
And keep my head wrapped modestly and seemly;
        She turns to RANNVEIG.
I must be humble—as one who lives on others.
        *She snatches off her wimple, slipping her
          gold circlet as she does so, and loosens
          her hair.*
Unless I may be hooded delicately
And use the adornment noble women use
I'll mock you with my flown young widowhood,
Letting my hair go loose past either cheek
In two bright clouds and drop beyond my bosom,
Turning the waving ends under my girdle
As young glad widows do, and as I did
Ere ever you saw me—ay, and when you found
    me
And met me as a king meets a queen
In the undying light of a summer night
With burning robes and glances—stirring the
    heart with scarlet.
        *She ticks the long ends of her hair under
          her girdle.*

THE RIDING TO LITHEND

RANNVEIG.

You have cast the head-ring of the nobly nurtured,
Being eager for a bold uncovered head.
You are conversant with a widow's fancies. . . .
Ay, you are ready with your widowhood:
Two men have had you, chilled their bosoms with
    you,
And trusted that they held a precious thing—
Yet your mean passionate wastefulness poured out
Their lives for joy of seeing something done with.
Cannot you wait this time? 'Twill not be long.

HALLGERD.

I am a hazardous desirable thing,
A warm unsounded peril, a flashing mischief,
A divine malice, a disquieting voice:
Thus I was shapen, and it is my pride
To nourish all the fires that mingled me.
I am not long moved, I do not mar my face,
Though men have sunk in me as in a quicksand.
Well, death is terrible. Was I not worth it?
Does not the light change on me as I breathe?
Could I not take the hearts of generations,
Walking among their dreams? O, I have might,
Although it drives me too and is not my own
    deed.
And Gunnar is great, or he had died long since.
It is my joy that Gunnar stays with me:
Indeed the offence is theirs who hunted him,
His banishment is not just; his wrongs increase,
His honour and his following shall increase
If he is steadfast for his blamelessness.

RANNVEIG.

Law is not justice, but the sacrifice

Of singular virtues to the dull world's ease of
    mind;
It measures men by the most vicious men;
It is a bargaining with vanities,
Lest too much right should make men hate each
    other
And hasten the last battle of all the nations.
Gunnar should have kept the atonement set,
For then those men would turn to other quarrels.

GUNNAR.
I know not why it is I must be fighting,
For ever fighting, when the slaying of men
Is a more weary and aimless thing to me
Than most men think it . . . and most women too.
There is a woman here who grieves she loves me,
And she too must be fighting me for ever
With her dim ravenous unsated mind. . .
Ay, Hallgerd, there's that in her which desires
Men to fight on for ever because she lives:
When she took form she did it like a hunger
To nibble earth's lip away until the sea
Poured down the darkness. Why then should I
    sail
Upon a voyage that can end but here?
She means that I shall fight until I die:
Why must she be put off by whittled years,
When none can die until his time has come?
               He turns to the hound by the fire.
Samm, drowsy friend, dost scent a prey in dreams?
Shake off thy shag of sleep and get to thy watch:
'Tis time to be our eyes till the next light.
Out, out to the yard, good Samm.
        He goes to the left, followed by the hound.
        In the meantime HALLGERD *has*

*seated herself in the high-seat near
the sewing-women, turning herself
away and tugging at a strand of her
hair, the end of which she bites.*

RANNVEIG, *intercepting him.*

                    Nay, let me take him.
It is not safe—there may be men who hide
Hallgerd, look up; call Gunnar to you there:

                  HALLGERD *is motionless.*
Lad, she beckons. I say you shall not come.

GUNNAR, *laughing.*
Fierce woman, teach me to be brave in age,
And let us see if it is safe for you.

       He leads RANNVEIG *out, his hand on her
shoulder; the hound goes with them.*

STEINVOR.
Mistress, my heart is big with mutinies
For your proud sake: does not your heart mount
    up?
He is an outlaw now and could not hold you
If you should choose to leave him. Is it not law?
Is it not law that you could loose this marriage—
Nay, that he loosed it shamefully years ago
By a hard blow that bruised your innocent cheek,
Dishonouring you to lesser women and chiefs?
See, it burns up again at the stroke of thought.
Come, leave him, mistress; we will go with you.
There is no woman in the country now
Whose name can kindle men as yours can do—
Ay, many would pile for you the silks he grudges;
And if you did withdraw your potent presence
Fire would not spare this house so reverently.

95

HALLGERD.
Am I a wandering flame that sears and passes?
We must bide here, good Steinvor, and be quiet.
Without a man a woman cannot rule,
Nor kill without a knife; and where's the man
That I shall put before this goodly Gunnar?
I will not be made less by a less man.
There is no man so great as my man Gunnar:
I have set men at him to show forth his might;
I have planned thefts and breakings of his word
When my pent heart grew sore with fermentation
Of malice too long undone, yet could not stir him.
O, I will make a battle of the Thing,
Where men vow holy peace, to magnify him.
Is it not rare to sit and wait o' nights,
Knowing that murderousness may even now
Be coming down outside like second darkness
Because my man is greater?

STEINVOR, *shuddering.*   Is it not rare.

HALLGERD.
That blow upon the face
So long ago is best not spoken of.
I drave a thrall to steal and burn at Otkell's
Who would not sell to us in famine time
But denied Gunnar as if he were suppliant:
Then at our feast when men rode from the Thing
I spread the stolen food and Gunnar knew.
He smote me upon the face . . . indeed he smote
    me. . . .
O, Gunnar smote me and had shame of me
And said he'd not partake with any thief;
Although I stole to injure his despiser . . .
But if he had abandoned me as well

THE RIDING TO LITHEND

'Tis I who should have been unmated now;
For many men would soon have judged me thief
And shut me from this land until I died—
And then I should have lost him. . . . Yet he
    smote me. . . .

ASTRID.
He kept you his—yes, and maybe saved you
From a debasement that could madden or kill,
For women thieves ere now have felt a knife
Severing ear or nose. And yet the feud
You sowed with Otkell's house shall murder
    Gunnar.
Otkell was slain: then Gunnar's enviers,
Who could not crush him under his own horse
At the big horse-fight, stirred up Otkell's son
To avenge his father; for should he be slain
Two in one stock would prove old Njal's fore-
    telling,
And Gunnar's place be emptied either way
For those high helpless men who cannot fill it.
O, mistress, you have hurt us all in this:
You have cut off your strength, you have maimed
    yourself,
You are losing power and worship and men's trust.
When Gunnar dies no other man dare take you.

HALLGERD.
You gather poison in your mouth for me.
A high-born woman may handle what she fancies
Without being ear-pruned like a pilfering beggar.
Look to your ears if you touch ought of mine:
Ay, you shall join the mumping sisterhood
And tramp and learn your difference from me.
        She turns from ASTRID.
Steinvor, I have remembered the great veil,

97   H

THE RIDING TO LITHEND

The woven cloud, the tissue of gold and garlands,
That Gunnar took from some outlandish ship
And deemed a thing from Greekland or from Hind:
Fetch it from the ambry in the bower.
> STEINVOR *goes out by the daïs door*

ASTRID.
Mistress, indeed you are a cherished woman.
That veil is worth a lifetime's weight of coifs:
I have heard a queen offered her daughter for it,
But Gunnar said it should come home and wait—
And then gave it to you. The half of Iceland
Tells fabulous legends of a fabulous thing,
Yet never saw it: I know they never saw it,
For ere it reached the ambry I came on it
Tumbled in the loft with ragged kirtles.

HALLGERD.
What, are you there again? Let Gunnar alone.
> STEINVOR *enters with the veil folded.*
> HALLGERD *takes it with one hand*
> *and shakes it into a heap.*

This is the cloth. He brought it out at night,
In the first hour that we were left together,
And begged of me to wear it at high feasts
And more outshine all women of my time:
He shaped it to my head with my gold circlet,
Saying my hair smouldered like Rhine-fire
      through,
He let it fall about my neck and fall
About my shoulders, mingle with my skirts
And billow in the draught along the floor.
> *She rises and holds the veil behind her head.*
I know I dazzled as if I entered in
And walked upon a windy sunset and drank it,

98

Yet must I stammer at such strange uncouth-
    ness
And tear it from me, tangling my arms in it—
I could not so befool myself and seem
A laughable bundle in each woman's eyes,
Wearing such things as no one ever wore,
Useless . . . no head-cloth . . . too unlike my
    fellows.
Yet he turns miser for a tiny coif.
It would cut into many golden coifs
And dim some women in their Irish clouts—
But no; I'll shape and stitch it into shifts,
Smirch it like linen, patch it with rags, to watch
His silent anger when he sees my answer.
Give me thy shears, girl Oddny.

ODDNY.   You'll not part it?

HALLGERD.
I'll shorten it.

ODDNY.   I have no shears with me.

HALLGERD.
No matter; I can start it with my teeth
And tear it down the folds. So. So. So. So.
Here's a fine shift for summer: and another.
I'll find my shears and chop out waists and neck-
    holes.
Ay, Gunnar, Gunnar!
       She throws the tissue on the ground, and
         goes out by the daïs door

ODDNY, *lifting one of the pieces.*
        O me! A wonder has vanished.

STEINVOR.
What is a wonder less? She has done finely,
Setting her worth above dead marvels and
    shows. . . .

> *The deep menacing baying of the hound is
> heard near at hand. A woman's cry
> follows it.*

They come, they come! Let us flee by the bower!

> *Starting up, she stumbles in the tissue and
> sinks upon it. The others rise.*

You are leaving me—will you not wait for me—
Take, take me with you. . . .

> *Mingled cries of women are heard.*

GUNNAR, *outside.*   Samm, it is well: be still.
Women, be quiet; loose me; get from my feet,
Or I will set the hound to wipe me clear. . . .

STEINVOR, *recovering herself.*
Women are sent to spy.

> *The sound of a door being opened is heard.*
> GUNNAR *enters from the left, followed
> by three beggar-women,* BIARTEY,
> JOFRID, *and* GUDFINN. *They hobble
> and limp, and are swathed in shape-
> less nameless rags which trail about
> their feet;* BIARTEY'S *left sleeve is torn
> completely away, leaving her arm bare
> and mud-smeared; the others' skirts
> are torn, and* JOFRID'S *gown at the
> neck;* GUDFINN *wears a felt hood
> buttoned under her chin, the others'
> faces are almost hid in falling tangles
> of grey hair. Their faces are shrivelled
> and weather-beaten, and* BIARTEY'S

THE RIDING TO LITHEND

*mouth is distorted by two front teeth
that project like tusks.*

GUNNAR.   Get in to the light.
Yea, has he mouthed ye? . . . What men send
    ye here?
Who are ye? Whence come ye? What do ye seek?
I think no mother ever suckled you:
You must have dragged your roots up in waste
    places
One foot at once, or heaved a shoulder up—

BIARTEY, *interrupting him.*
Out of the bosoms of cairns and standing stones.
I am Biartey: she is Jofrid: she is Gudfinn:
We are lone women known to no man now.
We are not sent: we come.

GUNNAR.   Well, you come.
You appear by night, rising under my eyes
Like marshy breath or shadows on the wall;
Yet the hound scented you like any evil
That feels upon the night for a way out.
And do you, then, indeed wend alone?
Came you from the West or the sky-covering
    North,
Yet saw no thin steel moving in the dark?

BIARTEY.
Not West, not North: we slept upon the East,
Arising in the East where no men dwell.
We have abided in the mountain places,
Chanted our woes among the black rocks crouch-
    ing;
        GUDFINN *joins her in a sing-song utter-
        ance.*

THE RIDING TO LITHEND

From the East, from the East we drove and the
    wind waved us,
Over the heaths, over the barren ashes.
We are old, our eyes are old, and the light hurts us,
We have skins on our eyes that part alone to the
    star-light.
We stumble about the night, the rocks tremble
Beneath our trembling feet; black sky thickens,
Breaks into clots, and lets the moon upon us.

      JOFRID *joins her voice to the voices of the*
        other two.

Far from the men who fear us, men who stone us,
Hiding, hiding, flying whene'er they slumber,
High on the crags we pause, over the moon-gulfs;
Black clouds fall and leave us up in the moon-
    depths
Where wind flaps our hair and cloaks like fin-
    webs,
Ay, and our sleeves that toss with our arms and
    the cadence
Of quavering crying among the threatening
    echoes.
Then we spread our cloaks and leap down the
    rock-stairs,
Sweeping the heaths with our skirts, greying the
    dew-bloom,
Until we feel a pool on the wide dew stretches
Stilled by the moon or ruffling like breast-feathers,
And, with grey sleeves cheating the sleepy herons,
Squat among them, pillow us there and sleep.
But in the harder wastes we stand upright,
Like splintered rain-worn boulders set to the wind
In old confederacy, and rest and sleep.

      HALLGERD'S *women are huddled together*
      and clasping each other.

ODDNY.
What can these women be who sleep like horses,
Standing up in the darkness. . . . What will they
    do.

GUNNAR.
Ye wail like ravens and have no human thoughts.
What do ye seek? What will ye here with us?

BIARTEY, *as all three cower suddenly.*
Succour upon this terrible journeying.
We have a message for a man in the West,
Sent by an old man sitting in the East.
We are spent, our feet are moving wounds, our
    bodies
Dream of themselves and seem to trail behind us.
Because we went unfed down in the mountains.
Feed us and shelter us beneath your roof,
And put us over the Markfleet, over the channels.
We are weak old women : we are beseeching you.

GUNNAR.
You may bide here this night, but on the morrow
You shall go over, for tramping shameless women
Carry too many tales from stead to stead—
And sometimes heavier gear than breath and lies.
These women will tell the mistress all I grant you ;
Get to the fire until she shall return.

BIARTEY.
Thou art a merciful man and we shall thank thee.
       GUNNAR *goes out again to the left.*
      The old women approach the young ones
          gradually.
Little ones, do not doubt us. Could we hurt you?
Because we are ugly must we be bewitched?

THE RIDING TO LITHEND

STEINVOR.
Nay, but bewitch us.

BIARTEY.   Not in a litten house:
Not ere the hour when night turns on itself
And shakes the silence: not while ye wake to-
    gether.
Sweet voice, tell us, was that verily Gunnar?

STEINVOR.
Arrh—do not touch me, unclean flyer-by-night:
Have ye birds' feet to match such bat-webbed
    fingers?

BIARTEY.
I am only a cowed curst woman who walks with
    death;
I will crouch here. Tell us, was it Gunnar?

ODDNY.
Yea, Gunnar surely. Is he not big enough
To fit the songs about him?

BIARTEY.   He is a man.
Why will his manhood urge him to be dead?
We walk about the whole old land at night,
We enter many dales and many halls:
And everywhere is talk of Gunnar's greatness,
His slayings and his fate outside the law.
The last ship has not gone: why will he tarry?

ODDNY.
He chose a ship, but men who rode with him
Say that his horse threw him upon the shore,
His face toward the Lithe and his own fields;

THE RIDING TO LITHEND

As he arose he trembled at what he gazed on
(Although those men saw nothing pass or meet
    them)
And said   What said he, girls?

ASTRID.   " Fair is the Lithe:
So fair I never thought it was so fair.
Its corn is white, its meadows green after mowing.
I will ride home again and never leave it."

ODDNY.
'Tis an unlikely tale: he never said it.
No one could mind such things in such an hour.
Plainly he saw his fetch come down the sands,
And knew he need not seek another country
And take that with him to walk upon the deck
In night and storm.

GUDFINN.   He he he! No man speaks thus.

JOFRID.
No man, no man: he must be doomed somewhere.

BIARTEY.
Doomed and fey, my sisters. . . . We are too old,
Yet I'd not marvel if we outlasted him.
Sisters, that is a fair fierce girl who spins. . . .
My fair fierce girl, you could fight—but can you
    ride?
Would you not shout to be riding in a storm?
Ah . . . h, girls learnt riding well when I was a
    girl,
And foam rides on the breakers as I was taught. . . .
My fair fierce girl, tell me your noble name.

THE RIDING TO LITHEND

ODDNY.
My name is Oddny.

BIARTEY.   Oddny, when you are old
Would you not be proud to be no man's purse-
    string,
But wild and wandering and friends with the earth?
Wander with us and learn to be old yet living.
We'd win fine food with you to beg for us.

STEINVOR.
Despised, cast out, unclean, and loose men's
    night-bird.

ODDNY.
When I am old I shall be some man's friend,
And hold him when the darkness comes. . . .

BIARTEY.
And mumble by the fire and blink. . . .
Good Oddny, let me spin for you awhile,
That Gunnar's house may profit by his guesting:
Come, trust me with your distaff. . . .

ODDNY.   Are there spells
Wrought on a distaff?

STEINVOR.   Only by the Norns,
And they'll not sit with human folk to-night.

ODDNY.
Then you may spin all night for what I care;
But let the yarn run clean from knots and snarls,
Or I shall have the blame when you are gone.

BIARTEY, *taking the distaff.*
Trust well the aged knowledge of my hands;

THE RIDING TO LITHEND

Thin and thin do I spin, and the thread draws
    finer.

                    She sings as she spins.
      They go by three,
      And the moon shivers;
      The tired waves flee,
      The hidden rivers
      Also flee.

      I take three strands;
      There is one for her,
      One for my hands,
      And one to stir
      For another's hands.

      I twine them thinner,
      The dead wool doubts;
      The outer is inner,
      The core slips out. . . .
    HALLGERD *re-enters by the dais door,*
      holding a pair of shears.

HALLGERD.
What are these women, Oddny? Who let them in?

BIARTEY, *who spins through all that follows.*
Lady, the man of fame who is your man
Gave us his peace to-night, and that of his house.
We are blown beggars tramping about the land,
Denied a home for our evil and vagrant hearts;
We sought this shelter when the first dew soaked
    us,
And should have perished by the giant hound
But Gunnar fought it with his eyes and saved us.
That is a strange hound, with a man's mind in it.

THE RIDING TO LITHEND

HALLGERD, *seating herself in the high-seat.*
It is an Irish hound, from that strange soil
Where men by day walk with unearthly eyes
And cross the veils of the air, and are not men
But fierce abstractions eating their own hearts
Impatiently and seeing too much to be joyful. . .
If Gunnar welcomed ye, ye may remain.

BIARTEY.
She is a fair free lady, is she not?
But that was to be looked for in a high one
Who counts among her fathers the bright Sigurd,
The bane of Fafnir the Worm, the end of the god-
    kings;
Among her mothers Brynhild, the lass of Odin,
The maddener of swords, the night-clouds' rider.
She has kept sweet that father's lore of bird-speech,
She wears that mother's power to cheat a god.
Sisters, she does well to be proud

JOFRID AND GUDFINN.   Ay, well

HALLGERD, *shaping the tissue with her shears.*
I need no witch to tell I am of rare seed,
Nor measure my pride nor praise it. Do I not
    know?
Old women, ye are welcomed: sit with us,
And while we stitch tell us what gossip runs—
But if strife might be warmed by spreading it.

BIARTEY.
Lady, we are hungered; we were lost
All night among the mountains of the East;
Clouds of the cliffs come down my eyes again. . . .
I pray you let some thrall bring us to food.

THE RIDING TO LITHEND

HALLGERD.
Ye get nought here. The supper is long over;
The women shall not let ye know the food-house,
Or ye'll be thieving in the night. Ye are idle,
Ye suck a man's house bare and seek another.
'Tis bed-time; get to sleep—that stills much
    hunger.

BIARTEY.
Now it is easy to be seeing what spoils you.
You were not grasping or ought but over warm
When Sigmund, Gunnar's kinsman, guested here.
You followed him, you were too kind with him,
You lavished Gunnar's treasure and gear on him
To draw him on, and did not call that thieving.
Ay, Sigmund took your feuds on him and died
As Gunnar shall. Men have much harm by you.

HALLGERD.
Now have I gashed the golden cloth awry:
'Tis ended—a ruin of clouts—the worth of the
    gift—
Bridal dish-clouts—nay, a bundle of flame.
I'll burn it to a breath of its old queen's ashes:
Fire, O fire, drink up . . .
        She throws the shreds of the veil on the
        glowing embers: they waft to ashes
        with a brief high flare. She goes to
        JOFRID.
                There 's one of you
That holds her head in a bird's sideways fashion:
I know that reach o' the chin. . . . What's under
    thy hair?—
        She fixes JOFRID *with her knee, and lifts*
        her hair.

Pfui, 'tis not hair, but sopped and rotting moss—
A thief, a thief indeed.   . And twice a thief.
She has no ears. Keep thy hooked fingers still
While thou art here, for if I miss a mouthful
Thou shalt miss all thy nose. Get up, get up;
I'll lodge ye with the mares. . . .

JOFRID, *starting up.*   Three men, three men,
Three men have wived you, and for all you gave
    them
Paid with three blows upon a cheek once kissed—
To every man a blow—and the last blow
All the land knows was won by thieving food. . . .
Yea, Gunnar is ended by the theft and the thief.
Is it not told that when you first grew tall,
A false rare girl, Hrut your own kinsman said
" I know not whence thief's eyes entered our
    blood."
You have more ears, yet are you not my sister?
Our evil vagrant heart is deeper in you.

HALLGERD, *snatching the distaff from Biartey.*
Out and be gone, be gone. Lie with the moun-
    tains,
Smother among the thunder; stale dew mould you.
Outstrip the hound, or he shall so embrace
    you. . . .

BIARTEY.
Now is all done   all done   and all your
    deed!
She broke the thread, and it shall not join again.
Spindle, spindle, the coiling weft shall dwindle;
Leap on the fire and burn, for all is done
        *She casts the spindle upon the fire, and
        stretches her hands toward it.*

HALLGERD, *attacking them with the distaff.*
Into the night. . . . Dissolve.

BIARTEY, *as the three rush toward the door.*
                              Sisters, away·
Leave the woman to her smouldering beauty,
Leave the fire that's kinder than the woman,
Leave the roof-tree ere it falls. It falls.
                    GUDFINN *joins her. Each time Hallgerd*
                        flags they turn as they chant, and
                        point at her.
We shall cry no more in the high rock-places,
We are gone from the night the winds and the
    clouds are empty:
Soon the man in the West shall receive our
    message.
                    JOFRID'S *voice joins the other voices.*
Men reject us, yet their house is unstable. . . .
The slayers' hands are warm—the sound of their
    riding
Reached us down the ages, ever approaching.

HALLGERD, *at the same time, her voice high over*
    theirs.
Pack, ye rag-heaps—or I'll unravel you.

THE THREE, *continuously.*
House that spurns us, woe shall come upon you:
Death shall hollow you. Now we curse the
    woman—
May all the woes smite her till she can feel them.
Shall we not roost in her bower yet? Woe! Woe!
                    The distaff breaks, and Hallgerd drives
                        them out with her hands. Their voices
                        continue for a moment outside, dying
                        away.

THE RIDING TO LITHEND

Call to the owl-friends   Woe! Woe! Woe!

ASTRID.

Whence came these mounds of dread to haunt
    the night?
It doubles this disquiet to have them near us.

ODDNY.

They must be witches—and it was my distaff—
Will fire eat through me . . . .

STEINVOR.   Or the Norns themselves.

HALLGERD.

Or bad old women used to govern by fear.
To bed, to bed—we are all up too late.

STEINVOR, *as she turns with* ASTRID *and* ODDNY
    to the daïs.
If beds are made for sleep we might sit long.
              They go out by the daïs door

GUNNAR, *as he enters hastily from the left.*
Where are those women? There's some secret in
    them:
I have heard such others crying down to them.

HALLGERD.

They turned foul-mouthed, they beckoned evil
    toward us—
I drove them forth a breath ago.

GUNNAR.   Forth? Whence?

HALLGERD.

By the great door: they cried about the night.
         RANNVEIG *follows* GUNNAR *in.*

THE RIDING TO LITHEND

GUNNAR.
Nay, but I entered there and passed them not.
Mother, where are the women?

RANNVEIG.   I saw none come.

GUNNAR.
They have not come, they have gone.

RANNVEIG.   I crossed the yard,
Hearing a noise, but a big bird dropped past,
Beating my eyes; and then the yard was clear.
          *The deep baying of the hound is heard
          again.*

GUNNAR.
They must be spies: yonder is news of them.
The wise hound knew them, and knew them again.
          The baying is succeeded by one wild howl.
                              Nay, nay!
Men treat thee sorely, Samm my fosterling:
Even by death thou warnest—but it is meant
That our two deaths will not be far apart.

RANNVEIG.
Think you that men are yonder?

GUNNAR.   Men are yonder.

RANNVEIG.
My son, my son, get on the rattling war-woof,
The old grey shift of Odin, the hide of steel.
Handle the snake with edges, the fang of the
          rings.

GUNNAR, *going to the weapons by the high-seat.*
There are not enough moments to get under
That heavy fleece: an iron hat must serve . . .

113

THE RIDING TO LITHEND

HALLGERD.
O brave! O brave!—he'll dare them with no
    shield.

GUNNAR, *lifting down the great bill from the wall.*
Let me but reach this haft, I shall get hold
Of steel enough to fence me all about.
        *He shakes the bill above his head: a deep
        resonant humming follows.*
        The dais door is thrown open, and ODDNY,
        ASTRID, *and* STEINVOR *stream
        through in their night-clothes.*

STEINVOR.   The bill!

ODDNY.   The bill is singing!

ASTRID   The bill sings!

GUNNAR, *shaking the bill again.*
Ay, brain-biter, waken . . . Awake and whisper
Out of the throat of dread thy one brief burden.
Blind art thou, and thy kiss will do no choosing:
Worn art thou to a hair's grey edge, a nothing
That slips through all it finds, seeking more
    nothing.
There is a time, brain-biter, a time that comes
When there shall be much quietness for thee:
Men will be still about thee. I shall know.
It is not yet: the wind shall hiss at thee first.
Ahui! Leap up, brain-biter; sing again.
Sing! Sing thy verse of anger and feel my hands.

RANNVEIG.
Stand thou, my Gunnar, in the porch to meet them,
And the great door shall keep thy back for thee.

THE RIDING TO LITHEND

GUNNAR.
I had a brother there. Brother, where are you. . . .

HALLGERD.
Nay, nay. Get thou, my Gunnar, to the loft,
Stand at the casement, watch them how they come.
Arrows maybe could drop on them from there.

RANNVEIG.
'Tis good: the woman's cunning for once is
    faithful.

GUNNAR, *turning again to the weapons.*
'Tis good, for now I hear a foot that stumbles
Along the stable-roof against the hall.
My bow—where is my bow? Here with its
    arrows. . . .
Go in again, you women on the daïs,
And listen at the casement of the bower
For men who cross the yard, and for their words.

ASTRID.
O, Gunnar, we shall serve you.
        ASTRID, ODDNY, *and* STEINVOR *go out*
        by the daïs door.

RANNVEIG.   Hallgerd, come;
We must shut fast the door, bar the great door,
Or they'll be in on us and murder him.

HALLGERD.
Not I: I'd rather set the door wide open
And watch my Gunnar kindling at the peril,
Keeping them back—shaming men for ever
Who could not enter at a gaping door.

115

THE RIDING TO LITHEND

RANNVEIG.
Bar the great door, I say, or I will bar it—
Door of the house you rule. . .   Son, son,
     command it.

GUNNAR, *as he ascends to the loft.*
O, spendthrift fire, do you waft up again?
Hallgerd, what riot of ruinous chance will sate
     you? . . .
Let the door stand, my mother: it is her way.
               He looks out of the casement.
Here's a red kirtle on the lower roof.
          *He thrusts with the bill through the case-
          ment.*

A MAN'S VOICE, *far off.*   Is Gunnar within?

THORGRIM THE EASTERLING'S VOICE, *near the
     casement.*
                    Find that out for yourselves:
I am only sure his bill is yet within.
               A noise of falling is heard.

GUNNAR.
The Easterling from Sandgil might be dying—
He has gone down the roof, yet no feet helped him.
          A shouting of many men is heard: GUN-
               NAR *starts back from the casement as
               several arrows fly in.*
Now there are black flies biting before a storm.
I see men gathering beneath the cart-shed:
Gizur the White and Geir the priest are there,
And a lean whispering shape that should be Mord.
I have a sting for some one—
          He looses an arrow: a distant cry follows.
               Valgard's voice. .

THE RIDING TO LITHEND

A shaft of theirs is lying on the roof:
I'll send it back, for if it should take root
A hurt from their own spent and worthless weapon
Would put a scorn upon their tale for ever.

> *He leans out for the arrow.*

RANNVEIG.
Do not, my son: rouse them not up again
When they are slackening in their attack.

HALLGERD.
Shoot, shoot it out, and I'll come up to mock them.

GUNNAR, *loosing the arrow.*
Hoia! Swerve down upon them, little hawk.

> *A shot follows.*

Now they run all together round one man:
Now they murmur. . . .

A VOICE.   Close in, lift bows again:
He has no shafts, for this is one of ours.

> *Arrows fly in at the casement.*

GUNNAR.
Wife, here is something in my arm at last:
The head is twisted—I must cut it clear.

> STEINVOR *throws open the daïs door and*
> *rushes through with a high shriek.*

STEINVOR.
Woman, let us out—help us out—
The burning comes—they are calling out for fire.

> *She shrieks again.* ODDNY *and* ASTRID,
> *who have come behind her, muffle her*
> *head in a kirtle and lift her.*

ASTRID, *turning as they bear her out.*
Fire suffuses only her cloudy brain:
The flare she walks in is on the other side
Of her shot eyes. We heard a passionate voice,
A shrill unwomanish voice that must be Mord,
With "Let us burn him—burn him house and
    all."
And then a grave and trembling voice replied
" Although my life hung on it, it shall not be."
Again the cunning fanatic voice went on
" I say the house must burn above his head."
And the unlifted voice " Why wilt thou speak
Of what none wishes: it shall never be."
        ASTRID *and* ODDNY *disappear with*
        STEINVOR.

GUNNAR.
To fight with honest men is worth much friend-
    ship:
I'll strive with them again.
      He lifts his bow and loosens arrows at in
      tervals while HALLGERD *and* RANN-
      VEIG *speak.*

HALLGERD, *in an undertone to* RANNVEIG, *looking*
    out meanwhile to the left.
                Mother, come here—
Come here and hearken. Is there not a foot,
A stealthy step, a fumbling on the latch
Of the great door? They come, they come, old
    mother:
Are you not blithe and thirsty, knowing they come
And cannot be held back? Watch and be secret,
To feel things pass that cannot be undone.

RANNVEIG.
It is the latch. Cry out, cry out for Gunnar,
And bring him from the loft.

HALLGERD.   O, never:
For then they'd swarm upon him from the roof.
Leave him up there and he can bay both armies,
While the whole dance goes merrily before us
And we can warm our hearts at such a flare.

RANNVEIG, *turning both ways, while* HALLGERD
    watches her gleefully.
Gunnar, my son, my son! What shall I do.
        ORMILD *enters from the left, white and
            with her hand to her side, and walking
            as if she is sick.*

HALLGERD.
Bah—here's a bleached assault. . . .

RANNVEIG.   O, lonesome thing,
To be forgot and left in such a night.
What is there now—are terrors surging still?

ORMILD.
I know not what has gone: when the men came
I hid in the far cowhouse. I think I swooned . . .
And then I followed the shadow. Who is dead?

RANNVEIG.
Go to the bower: the women will care for you.
        ORMILD *totters up the hall from pillar to
            pillar.*

ASTRID, *entering by the daïs door.*
Now they have found the weather-ropes and lashed
    them

Over the carven ends of the beams outside:
They bear on them, they tighten them with levers,
And soon they'll tear the high roof off the hall.

GUNNAR.
Get back and bolt the women into the bower.
> ASTRID *takes* ORMILD, *who has just
> reached her, and goes out with her by
> the daïs door, which closes after them.*
Hallgerd, go in: I shall be here thereafter.

HALLGERD.
I will not stir. Your mother had best go in.

RANNVEIG.
How shall I stir?

VOICES, *outside and gathering volume.*
> Ai . . . Ai . . . Reach harder . . . Ai . . .

GUNNAR.
Stand clear, stand clear—it moves.

THE VOICES.   It moves   Ai, ai . . .
> *The whole roof slides down rumblingly,
> disappearing with a crash behind
> the wall of the house. All is dark
> above. Fine snow sifts down now and
> then to the end of the play.*

GUNNAR, *handling his bow.*
The wind has changed: 'tis coming on to snow.
The harvesters will hurry in to-morrow.
> THORBRAND THORLEIKSSON *appears
> above the wall-top a little past* GUN-
> NAR, *and, reaching noiselessly with a
> sword, cuts* GUNNAR'S *bowstring.*

120

THE RIDING TO LITHEND

GUNNAR, *dropping the bow and seizing his bill.*
Ay, Thorbrand, is it thou? That's a rare blade,
To shear through hemp and gut. . . . Let your
    wife have it
For snipping needle-yarn; or try it again.

THORBRAND, *raising his sword.*
I must be getting back ere the snow thickens:
So here's my message to the end—or farther.
Gunnar, this night it is time to start your journey
And get you out of Iceland. . . .

GUNNAR, *thristing at* THORBRAND *with the bill.*
                        I think it is:
So you shall go before me in the dark.
Wait for me when you find a quiet shelter.
        THORBRAND *sinks backward from the
        wall and is heard to fall farther.
        Immediately* ASBRAND THORLEIKS-
        SON *starts up in his place.*

ASBRAND, *striking repeatedly with a sword.*
O, down, down, down!

GUNNAR, *parrying the blows with the bill.*
               Ay, Asbrand, thou as well?
Thy brother Thorbrand was up here but now
He has gone back the other way, maybe—
Be hasty, or you'll not come up with him.
        He thrists with the bill: ASBRAND *lifts
        a shield before the blow.*
Here's the first shield that I have seen to-night.
        The bill pierces the shield: ASBRAND *dis-
        appears and is heard to fall.* GUNNAR
        turns from the casement.

THE RIDING TO LITHEND

Hallgerd, my harp that had but one long string,
But one low song, but one brief wingy flight,
Is voiceless, for my bowstring is cut off.
Sever two locks of hair for my sake now,
Spoil those bright coils of power, give me your
     hair,
And with my mother twist those locks together
Into a bowstring for me. Fierce small head,
Thy stinging tresses shall scourge men forth by
     me.

HALLGERD.
Does ought lie on it?

GUNNAR.   Nought but my life lies on it ;
For they will never dare to close on me
If I can keep my bow bended and singing.

HALLGERD, *tossing back her hair.*
Then now I call to your mind that bygone blow
You gave my face; and never a whit do I care
If you hold out a long time or a short.

GUNNAR.
Every man who has trod a war-ship's deck,
And borne a weapon of pride, has a proud heart
And asks not twice for any little thing.
Hallgerd, I'll ask no more from you, no more.

RANNVEIG, *tearing off her wimple.*
She will not mar her honour of widowhood.
O, widows' manes are priceless. . . . Off, mean
     wimple—
I am a finished widow, why do you hide me?
Son, son who knew my bosom before hers,

Look down and curse for an unreverend thing
An old bald woman who is no use at last.
These bleachy threads, these tufts of death's first
  combing,
And loosening heart-strings twisted up together
Would not make half a bowstring. Son, forgive
  me

GUNNAR.
A grasping woman's gold upon her head
Is made for hoarding, like all other gold:
A spendthrift woman's gold upon her head
Is made for spending on herself. Let be—
She goes her heart's way, and I go to earth.
          AUNUND'S *head rises above the wall near*
              GUNNAR.
What, are you there?

AUNUND.   Yes, Gunnar, we are here.

GUNNAR, *thrusting with the bill.*
Then bide you there.
          AUNUND'S *head sinks:* THORGEIR'S *rises*
              in the same place.
                    How many heads have you?

THORGEIR.
But half as many as the feet we grow on.

GUNNAR.
And I've not yet used up (*thrusting again*) all my
  hands.
          As he thrusts another man rises a little
              farther back, and leaps past him into
              the loft. Others follow, and GUNNAR

THE RIDING TO LITHEND

*is soon surrounded by many armed
men, so that only the rising and falling of his bill is seen.*

The threshing-floor is full. . . . Up, up, brain-
biter!
We work too late to-night—up, open the husks.
      O, smite and pulse
      On their anvil heads:
      The smithy is full,
      There are shoes to be made
      For the hoofs of the steeds
      Of the Valkyr girls. . . .

FIRST MAN.
      Hack through the shaft.

SECOND MAN.
      Receive the blade
      In the breast of a shield,
      And wrench it round. . .

GUNNAR.
      For the hoofs of the steeds
      Of the Valkyr girls
      Who race up the night
      To be first at our feast,
      First in the play
      With immortal spears
      In deadly holes.

THIRD MAN.
      Try at his back.

MANY VOICES, *shouting in confusion.*
Have him down. . . . Heels on the bill.   Ahui,
  ahui.   *The bill does not rise.*

THE RIDING TO LITHEND

HROALD, *with the breaking voice of a young man,*
high over all.
Father   It is my blow   It is I who kill
him. . . .
> *The crowd parts, suddenly silent, showing*
> GUNNAR *fallen.*
> RANNVEIG *covers her face with her hands.*

HALLGERD, *laughing as she leans forward and*
holds her breasts in her hands.
O, clear sweet laughter of my heart, flow out!
It is so mighty and beautiful and blithe
To watch a man dying—to hover and watch.

RANNVEIG.
Cease: are you not immortal in shame already?

HALLGERD.
Heroes, what deeds ye compass, what great
deeds—
One man has held ye from an open door:
Heroes, heroes, are ye undefeated?

GIZUR, *an old white-bearded man, to the other riders.*
We have laid low to earth a mighty chief:
We have laboured harder than on greater deeds,
And maybe won remembrance by the deeds
Of Gunnar when no deed of ours should live;
For this defence of his shall outlast kingdoms
And gather him fame till there are no more men.

MORD.
Come down and splinter those old birds his gods
That perch upon the carven high-seat pillars;
Wreck every place his shadow fell upon,
Rive out his gear, drive off his forfeit beasts.

THE RIDING TO LITHEND

SECOND MAN.
It shall not be.

MANY MEN.   Never.

GIZUR.   We'll never do it:
Let no man lift a blade or finger a clout—
Is not this Gunnar, Gunnar, whom we have slain?
Home, home, before the dawn shows all our
    deed.
> *The riders go down quickly over the wall-*
> *top, and disappear.*

HALLGERD.
Now I shall close his nostrils and his eyes,
And thereby take his blood-feud into my hands.

RANNVEIG.
If you do stir I'll choke you with your hair.
I will not let your murderous mind be near him
When he no more can choose and does not know.

HALLGERD.
His wife I was, and yet he never judged me:
He did not set your motherhood between us.
Let me alone—I stand here for my sons.

RANNVEIG.
The wolf, the carrion bird, and the fair woman
Hurry upon a corpse, as if they think
That all is left for them the grey gods need not.
> *She twines her hands in Hallgerd's hair*
> *and draws her down to the floor.*
O, I will comb your hair with bones and thumbs,
Array these locks in my right widow's way,

And deck you like the bed-mate of the dead.
Lie down upon the earth as Gunnar lies,
Or I can never match him in your looks
And whiten you and make your heart as cold.

HALLGERD.
Mother, what will you do? Unloose me now
Your eyes would not look so at me alone.

RANNVEIG.
Be still, my daughter . . .

HALLGERD.   And then?

RANNVEIG.   Ah, do not fear—
I see a peril nigh and all its blitheness.
Order your limbs—stretch out your length of
    beauty,
Let down your hands and close those deepening
    eyes,
Or you can never stiffen as you should.
A murdered man should have a murdered wife
When all his fate is treasured in her mouth.
This wifely hair-pin will be sharp enough.

HALLGERD, *starting up as* RANNVEIG *half loosens
    her to take a hair-pin from her own head.*
She is mad, mad   O, the bower is barred—
Hallgerd, come out, let mountains cover you...
                    She rushes out to the left.

RANNVEIG, *following her.*
The night take you indeed

THE RIDING TO LITHEND

GIZUR *enters from the left.*

GIZUR.   Ay, drive her out;
For no man's house was ever better by her.

RANNVEIG.
Is an old woman's life desired as well?

GIZUR.
We ask that you will grant us earth hereby
Of Gunnar's earth, for two men dead to-night
To lie beneath a cairn that we shall raise.

RANNVEIG.
Only for two? Take it: ask more of me.
I wish the measure were for all of you.

GIZUR.
Your words must be forgiven you, old mother,
For none has had a greater loss than yours.
Why would he set himself against us all .
                              He goes out.

RANNVEIG.
Gunnar, my son, we are alone again.
         She goes up the hall, mounts to the loft,
              and stoops beside him.
O, they have hurt you . . . but that is forgot.
Boy, it is bedtime; though I am too changed,
And cannot lift you up and lay you in,
You shall go warm to bed—I'll put you there.
There is no comfort in my breast to-night:
But close your eyes beneath my fingers' touch,
Slip your feet down, and let me smooth your
     hands;

Then sleep and sleep. Ay, all the world 's asleep;
But some will waken.   *She rises.*
You had a rare toy when you were awake—
I'll wipe it with my hair . . . Nay, keep it so,
The colour on it now has gladdened you.
It shall lie near you.
          She raises the bill: the deep hum follows.
                    No; it remembers him,
And other men shall fall by it through Gunnar:
The bill, the bill is singing . . . The bill sings!
          *She kisses the weapon, then shakes it on
          high.*

CURTAIN.

MIDSUMMER EVE

TO

CLINTON BALMER
AND THE DEAR MEMORY OF
JAMES HAMILTON HAY
FOR THE SUMMER OF 1900
AT CARTMEL

PERSONS:

NAN
BET
URSEL } Kitchen and Dairy Girls.
MAUDLIN
LIB

ROGER, a Carter.
MEASE, a Cowherd.

MIDSUMMER EVE

*The scene is the interior of an old barn on a knoll,
a long time ago. At the back the barn's doors
are opened widely; outside, a road rises slightly
from left to right in front of the barn; beyond
this the knoll sinks softly yet swiftly to a great
meadow, and thence to a wide rich valley of
more meadows and ever more meadows with
ancient large cherry and crab and sloe and
bullace and damson trees in their hedges whence
the white and pink thorn-blossom clots are not
quite gone, and of pastures shaded by tall clus-
tering trees. Afar the valley ceases in low,
densely wooded hills.*

*A late June twilight is deepening; a faint
moist heat-haze hides nothing, only distin-
guishing the planes of the distant trees with a
cloudy delicacy. There is no wind, nor any
movement; one blackbird sings somewhere for
a little while, then it ceases and there is no
sound in the fields.*

*The whole prospect is of a solitary, fruitfully
overgrown valley shut in from everywhere.*

*Within the barn, to the left, is a high hay-
mow with a ladder leaning against it; much
hay has been tumbled at its foot in forking from
the carts. To the right is a space of floor where
the corn is to be heaped in the ending of summer:*

as yet, however, it is empty, save for a wooden plough, a homely rough wooden roller, wooden harrows, an uptilted, pleasantly shaped cart whence the hay-shelvings have not yet been removed. In the far corner of the bare walls of undressed stone at this side is an open door leading into a mistal. Presently a cow is heard moaning sickly beyond this door.

The barn is still more dim than the land, so that a stretch of soft brown darkness is all that is known of the far-off roof. Nearing footfalls are heard in the road, and a woman's singing grows clearer

H OU, Hou," went the neatherd moaning
   Down along by the pasture's side;
He turned the cows at the midden-yard loaning,
   The loitering cows in the brown owl-tide:
Pale rose the last one, munching, droning,
   With wet grass stains on her udder and hide.

My lantern's rings to the low balks floated
   As Whitey's tail shook the mistal-sneck;
When I laid my cheek to her belly spotted
   I felt her honey-strong breath i' my neck,
For she turns her head does the curd-dark throated
   To watch my mouth start her teats with a peck.

        NAN, BET and URSEL ascend the road to
          the left and enter the barn as NAN
          ceases singing.
        They are white-hooded, clumsily shod,
          gownless; in the right hand NAN
          carries a willow frail, the others stone-
          ware greybeards; each holds several
          hay-rakes on her left shoulder.

MIDSUMMER EVE

URSEL.
September, O, September's in the song—
I will not have September in my heart,
The ending of so much deliciousness,
The year's sad luscious over-ripening.
Yet here's the haysel done with: how it hurt
To rake behind the last dim cart; and now
My soul creeps in me like the low pale night-
    mist
To know that in a moment past this moment
We shall not hear it slowly any more
Down in the lane where, wisping the close trees,
It follows us like a mournful sound of change.
Although the Summer is but newly kindled,
Tiptoe I over-reach the joy of it
(Ah, little perfect weeks of fruitfulness)
Because I tremble lest it be slipping past me
Before my eagerness will let me feel it.
Must joy for me be ever in things gone? . . .

NAN, *as they set down their burdens to lean the
    rakes against the wall, where four flails are
    hung, on the left of the door.*
Nay, there is comfort in the rainy nights,
The long moist twilights of the cider time
When girls hold fitful talk sat in the press-spot
Among the hid sweet apple heaps that gleam
In firelight to a humming out of doors
Of soddening water oozing down the soil;
And there is comfort too at Candlemas
From looking through the casement in the dark,
The last thing ere you chafe your toes in bed,
On the crisp quiet of the woods and fields,
Wondering if 'tis snow or all the moonlight,
Peering so anxiously along the wall

That shades still ewes and whiter first-dropped
    lambs. . . .
Ay, but I'm tired, lasses, tired now
Because the haysel's over and 'twas fair
And the land's savour wears me with delight.
I'm for indoors and resting—and, beside,
I'm fainest of my supper o' baking days.

BET.
Let all times slip to haste the barley week,
For then our nearest dancing-time will ripen . . .
But I'm for bed to get me doffed and stripped
To pick much grass seed from my smock and coats.

URSEL.
Listen, Bet; no cool sheets are yours to-night.
The milk-eyed goodies with grey loose-skinned
    throats,
Who maunder of rarer girlhoods none can prove,
Tell that at midnight on Midsummer-Eves
They waked in some lone shade far from all
    sleepers
To feel which should be wedded within the year;
For the year's unknown husbands' images
Come then like swoons from some where . . . ay,
    from some where.
Thoughts shaping for their women's heedless
    souls,
And if a maid will watch she sees her own
And knows her own, seeing her own alone,
Peering unseen as breath is in June nights.
Surely such dainties filled no cow-slow eyes;
But Nan and I mean watching and have bid
Maudlin at Grassgarth, Lib at Appletoft
Under our breath, and hither they steal this eve.

MIDSUMMER EVE

We knew we must not tell you ere the hour,
Or . . . or . . . too many hinds might creep to be
Their own drowsed leering loutish prophecies.

BET.
Am I so old or wistful to be ringed
That I must feign to be content with one?
Where is this moon-swayed peeping, then, to be,
This blest eavesdropping on a mood of fate?

NAN.
Here in the barn, where we may crouch un-
  thought-of
By moon-estrangèd eyes in gradual darkness.
And lest we startle at o'er-expected footfalls
Or with night-carried voices rouse the farm,
Maudlin and Lib will warn us by dove-cooings—
Sometimes I hear a cooing up warm nights
From dove pairs far too wise to be asleep,
But mistress bides awake for no such music.

BET.
Dove-cooing Lib will be a thing to brood on—
I'll miss nought here, although you count me
  least.

NAN.
All works with us; for at the forenoon drinking
I heard dame Stir-Wench mutter "These kesh-
  pithed lasses
Shall sleep no longer three-a-bed beneath
The dark damp closeness of the garret thatch,
That nigh their heads leans low upon the floor,
Until this heat is past; or they will grow
Yet more slob-cheeked and sodden and dough-
  limbed—

MIDSUMMER EVE

I never saw maids look more like green sickness."
And then she bade Giles carry our gear and bed-
    ding
Into the empty meal-webbed granary.
Nought could have fallen better; now we have
No moaning ladder's and open doors' groped
    passing,
No stocking feet need pad the dairy flags;
Only a silverly weathered latchless board
Keeps out the bats that flap toward pale shapes,
And waits to let us into the large night
Throughout the holiest of the mothering year.

BET.
She said green sickness but she meant green
    apples.
The codlin tree that e'er each moonset stretches
A creeping spider-shadow on the gable
Fills out its fruit weeks earlier this year,
And the one bough with apples onion-roped
Is one the mended ladder will not reach;
It is weight-arched against our garret window,
So that the curled leaves finger on the panes
When midnight winds are sturdy enough to lift it;
Mam Pantry knows and fears bare orchard-shelves
And herds us to an outhouse. Girls, those apples
Will all be basketed before their time,
Ere threshing heaps the granary once more
And sharp nights make her yield our loft again
Because she finds us cuddled on its threshold.

URSEL.
Mam Patch-Waist counts more eggs than four—
    she knows
Spring wenches' whifts let loose to sniff the night;

MIDSUMMER EVE

So straightway to the granary Mease she sped
To oil the lock and drive a staple in.
Small is our chance of watching now. . . .

NAN.   Quick-Pattens
Even ere she rounded must have been a likely,
A very likely maid for her to know
Our scapemell moods howe'er we prim our mouths.

BET.
Mease for two kisses left the staple loose.

URSEL, *laughing with* NAN.
Ay, Bet's the market woman, to be sure.

BET.
Mouths, even as eyes, were made to earn our wills.

NAN.
But how came Bet near Mease up in the corn-spot?
And if she knows the need o' the staple loose
Why will she care to watch with us to-night?

BET.
To learn which one it is, Nanikin sly.

NAN.
Had it been Mease he'd not have chaffered
        kisses
You know more now than you will learn to-night,
You will wed more than all we see to-night—
We shall win nought beyond a secret spice
Of unclipt gossip in a tasty hour. .
        A loitering dull sound is heard of cart
            wheels and horse-hooves out in the lane.

141

MIDSUMMER EVE

URSEL.
Hush, Nan—here come the lads. . . .

> *They lift their burdens, and stand aside
> for the cart to enter the barn; but as
> it comes in sight it passes along the
> road from the left to the right. It is
> piled with a roped load of hay;* ROGER
> *and* MEASE, *in long smocks and flap-
> ping hats, knee-breeches and ribbed
> stockings, accompany it,* ROGER *lead-
> ing the horse,* MEASE *holding to the
> shelvings behind with one hand and
> with the other slanting several hay-
> forks and a scythe against his
> shoulder.*

URSEL, *continuing.*   What, Roger, Mease
Why bring you not the cart and top the mow,
To feel in each limb's ebb hay harvest's spent?

ROGER, *halting.*
As we trailed up from Pear-tree Dale past Sheep-
    mires
Under a thick dew-breath we seemed to steal
As 'tween chill bed-clothes in December nights;
Into the load it soaked two fingers' length,
So now we needs must throw it off and spread it
To wait to-morrow's sun out in the yard
Ere it is ripe to top the sweating stack.

MEASE.
Moreover, we are wetter than the crop;
Wherefore be homing, russet-apple-faces,
To take our smocks and dry them off while we
Drink the mulled cider you are going to make.

142

MIDSUMMER EVE

URSEL.
Come, maids, we'd best get in ere mistress seeks
    us—
Beside, the longer we do loiter here
The longer shall we hold the house from sleep;
There's bowl and bucket rinsing to be done
And supper to set out if we would eat it.
Be neither meek nor eager in your toil,
Or Mother Dish-Clout in our gust will read
Some deed afoot; we'll wrangle sluggishly
Until she drives us off to bed unwashed.
Then, though we hear the lock shoot and her steps
Sink down the out-stair as she dips the key
Down the long pocket of her petticoat,
Do nought but cast your shoes—there's but one
    wall
Between her chamber and the granary—
Lie dim along the bed, and never whisper;
But, when we hear her bed-stocks creak and know
Her ears are well tied up beneath her night-cap,
Out slip Bet's staple and ourselves as well.
Seek the pale hollyhocks across the garden
(They glimmer a little in all Summer darkness),
And touch behind the hive-house shadow-
    hung

NAN.
And in the barn make happiness till dawn.

BET.
Dare we lie still, inside the dark, and wait
In such suppression for such unknown things?

MIDSUMMER EVE

As Bet *speaks they leave the barn to the*
right; Nan *resumes her song faintly*
and more faintly.

Nan.

Dusked seemed the eve as the cows trod in
   Under the roof-drip each to her stalling;
Full udders crusht shagged thighs between
   Were warm to my hands in the chill air's palling;
And through the wind's drifting of leaves yet green
   " Hou, hou," neared the neatherd's calling.
                  The song ceases in the distance.

Roger *turns into the barn with* Mease's *bundle*
   of hay-forks, and lays them in the empty cart
   as he sings.
I get no sleep in lambing nights,
   My woman gets no sleep;
      We fold the ewes if we sniff a thaw,
      And when they yean as we crouch i' their
        straw
She takes the lambs by our horn-fogged lights
   While I do handle the sheep.
          Footsteps are heard within the neat-house.

Roger, *calling through the neat-house door.*
Is the sick beast grown easier by now?

Mease, *entering from the neat-house.*
Poor Dapple-Back, milk fever 's bad on her.
'Twas her first calf and though 'twas smoothly
   dropped
She could not gather, but heaped a shapeless flank
Like a maid swooning; when the farrier came
" She'll die, she'll die," he said. " She'll not,"
   said I:
But nothing served at first—her slackened fell

MIDSUMMER EVE

Dried hard and never any sweat would stir,
The udder turned a dull and shivering white;
Yet now her ears twitch up to greet my voice,
The hide-hair moistens and the udder shrinks.
There'll be no need to wake with her to-night—
I'll not unwrap her till an hour ere dawn.
Come through and look at her as we wend in...
When you got up the cider for the meadows
Was there a butt still left?

ROGER, *as they go into the mistal together.*
                      Surely there was;
But the girls say she'll make it wait till harvest.
I never hired to any stead before
Where last year's cider trickled into June
          *All is soundless again save for the cow's
          moaning. The twilight deepens no
          farther, and presently its dead gold
          brownness becomes cooler in tone; the
          mist, which had been merged in the
          nightfall's dimness, imperceptibly be-
          comes apparent again, being suffused
          by an oozing of silveriness through the
          pervading brownness; moon-rise is
          evident, although the moon is hidden
          by the permeating mist which it fills.
          Perhaps a crying of bats is heard,
          but this is not certain. An owl cries
          somewhere—probably from one of the
          gable-holes, for it sounds both inside
          and outside at once; after many ten-
          tative Tu-whits it launches a full
          Tu-whoo and swings out far and low
          across the valley: a chirping of frogs
          begins in the nearest ditches.*

MIDSUMMER EVE

*A closer sound stills all these, being evi-
dently that of a woman's voice feign-
ing dove-notes; it ceases, light cautious
hurried steps are heard; it sounds
again, Maudlin slips round the door
corner to the left and enters the barn.
She is white-capped, her gown skirt
is bunched about her waist, her
bodice sleeves are turned back beyond
her elbows.*

MAUDLIN.
Nan ... Ursel ... Nan   Lib   Appletoft
    Lib, hast come?
There's no one here—I wish they might forget
And sleep, and let me feel a little lonely.
I need much loneliness wherein to suckle
The sadness that alone can bring content:
I am too burdened by long laughing days,
And as I wavered through this solemn vapour
Of the worn earth, the comfort-smelling earth,
Where unexpected trees rose wearily
And sank again like ashen-bosomed sighs,
I felt a new, delighting mournfulness
That made me know where I am sensitive
To the deep things of life; even the late May-
    bloom,
That stays the tiring Spring in this strange valley,
Loses its too self-conscious hope to-night—
The pink would fain be white, and the spent white
Still fog and sink to the moon and make an end.
I must be much alone in sorrowful nights.
I should have ease if Summer would but go,
Its green-lit glory fail; I am so eager
For overgrown too-mellowness loth to pass,

MIDSUMMER EVE

For dripping trees o'er soft decaying grass,
Bare orchards and shorn meadows and stripped
    gardens,
Brown cloudy woods that drooping mists make
    taller
About washed fields and muffled hills, subduing
All to a low remote romance and charm
Yet soon with other maids I may behold
A change that comes to snirp these buds in me. . . .
> *She lays herself on her back among the tum
> bled hay; soon she sings in a low voice*

Fetch the porridge pot hither to me,
The porridge pot and the dairy key,
And bring me a clout to wind my hair
Or the swarming bees will tangle there:
They drip from the hive in the orchard long,
And coil the green-cherried boughs among
As they follow the tanking tune I ring
Under the cherry leaves' shivering . .
They settle, they knit—come Ailce with the
    skep—
Step along, Mistyhead—Smearycap, step—
Steady it while I draw the bough
Warily down and shake it . . . Now. . . .
> *After a little silence she resumes.*

The maids went down to dip in the pool
When the mirrored moon had cooled the water;
But they never told the farmer's daughter,
For they knew she would tell her mother, the
    fool,
That the girls were out
And awaking the water,
With never a clout
Though the night was cool.
> *She hums the latter melody a little while.*

MIDSUMMER EVE

Without premonition URSEL, NAN *and*
BET *enter singly and noiselessly from
the right, each holding a hand of
the one before her. They are hood-
less, white-capped, and barelegged
now.*

URSEL, *in a low voice.*
I bade them hide until we came.   Lib
    Maudlin

MAUDLIN, *sitting up.*
Lib is not here: there's no one nigh at all;
And in the lanes nought moves but squirrel
    whifts,
Save that long gazing into the green darkness
Seems to show boles half stirred by creeping light
Amid the darker dark of trees impending.

BET.
Was it not Lib who was dew-drenched last harvest,
Hid in a wheat stook till she fell asleep?

NAN, *as they all seat themselves by* MAUDLIN.
Could any watch you as you slipped away?

MAUDLIN.
Our lambs and three fat beasts must take the road
Ere dawn to reach the morrow's far-off fair;
So I said I would sleep along the settle
And set the hinds their drinking ere they trudge.
None smelt me, but I must start home by
    three.
What is the moaning through that little door?

URSEL, *in alarm.*
I had forgot the beast; will Mease sleep with her?
148

MIDSUMMER EVE

NAN.
When I came in to milk soon after seven
He said the deathly loosening was pinched
And we should keep her without more sitting
    up.
Yet—the other cows pushed in and nosed her
As cows will do to helpless dying things
To MAUDLIN.

A heifer has milk fever.

MAUDLIN, *rising eagerly.*   Let me look—
I have not touched milk fever once, nor seen it·
I want to know what sense it can be like,
I am made to know with what sick thought it
    takes them,
To watch it wane and learn to handle it.
Ah, let me feel her, Nan, dear Nannie. .

NAN.   Nay.
The neat-house door is open on her stall
And hints the pool out in the yard beyond
Dreaming a dew-dull wash of unborn moonlight
In darkness sinkingly close as a bat's coat,
And the large stillness of her weary eyes
Might image that   although we should not
    see her. . .

MAUDLIN.
I know, I know. . . . But we can shut our eyes—
Nay, fear would lift them—let us enter blindfold;
My fingers know just what they ought to do.

BET.
Nay, she might die . . . I saw a cow die once:
She tried to turn her head across her shoulder

149

And looked at me as if 'twas all my doing,
Then laid it down again with a straight throat . . .
I fear for that old wrong I never did. . .

> *A deep-voiced woman is heard making low*
> *dove-sounds.*

Comes Lib.

> *They rise to meet the new comer, but draw*
> *back half in laughter, half in uneasy*
> *amazement as she appears to the left.*
> *She is stockinged and shod, but her*
> *topmost apparel is nightgown and*
> *nightcap.*

BET, *continuing.*

    Lib   Lib   is she asleep or dead?

LIB, *entering the barn.*
Do I not seem the shadow of a husband?
Am I too late? I could not choose my coming:
'Tis churning day to-morrow, and nought would
    serve
The old one but that we must scald the churn
And wipe the cream-pots' lips and set them nigh
Before we slept—she was so cross because
One cow had broken, one cast before its time,
Some hens had laid away, farmer had blamed her
For standing over us to make us strip
The cows too hard; so she was queer with us.
That kept us late from bed, and when at last
Our fallen skirts were cooling on the floor
I had to lay me down beside Ruth
Until she slept; for Candle-Face tells tales—
'Twas she who lost us the low garden-chamber
Where hang the dry sweet herbs, and earned
    instead

MIDSUMMER EVE

One with a lattice up against the stars,
By peaching of my clambering through the case-
        ment
'Mid dropping plums that night I went some-
        where;
But when I heard her wet mouth on the pillow
I left her, stuffed my coats within my arm
And out along the landing. As I neared
The old one's chamber-door a warped board
        chirped,
My limbs went loose and motionless with fear;
On I slid again and down the stairs,
And in the kitchen found I had no raiment.
I dared not grope for it nor make a light;
So two unmended stockings on the settle,
My shoes upon the hearth, were all I had:
But in the warm night it was comforting
To feel myself half indistinguishable
From the grey, stirless oats I stood among,
Or the evasive gleams and thinner places
Of mist-lit woodlands, or from slim birch boles;
And when a woman met me by the brook
I was so pale and slow she ran from me.
                The others laugh as they lead her to
                crouch with them in the hay.
Why is there moaning through that little door?

NAN.
A heifer has milk fever.   *There is a silence.*

LIB, *in a low voice.*   Women have that. . . .
Why are we thankful for a deal of trouble? . . .
My sister Jen was pleased and proud with herself;
And when her second obedience came to her
She was well eased—but goody Slippy-Stockings,

Who went for wisdom-dame, bore the hot jug
Too brimmed when it was time to draw the
    milk. . . .
They had to dry the milk, and it, being eager,
Went the wrong way and oozed into her head:
The little one died so soon. She lay there
Sooing the oldest milking-croon of all—
    "Baby calf-lips nuzzle not nigh you,
    'Tis my fingers firm that try you
      Knowingly;
    Patch-Eye, Teaty, I'll not wry you,
    Let your warm milk down to me. . . ."
Then she would wear her wedding gown all night,
And in the orchard we could hear her sing
Mall, go, gather a Posy—Lasses turn Grey—
Wander, Wonder—and, Peg was clouting her
    Nightcaps;
She sank heavily to uneasy stillness,
Then mooed a baby-noise; till, the fourth dawn,
She hollowed her arms gently across her body,
"Cold, cold," she said, and then "Cover us
    up" . . .
And she grew colder. . . .

MAUDLIN.   Much strangeness comes in it:
I've wondered what there is in me to gather
So secretly, why life can leak such whiteness,
And if we feel it change, and how in it
We sow hid things that never were in us—
Can it be that our thoughts go into it,
And all we feel and see must alter it
From white to white that seems but white to us?
I knew a woman and her daughter once
Who went together. . . . The young one's died;
    she cried,

O she did cry, until the mother said
"Here, lass, have mine; I know, and you shall
    know."
Girls, she did that quite calmly: ere he would take,
Mab had to cover his eyes with a warm cloth,
And even o' nights to wear her mother's clothes.
'Tis grave to suckle across the brood like that—
It threads the mind. . . .

BET.   Mothering, mothering, mothering—
Cannot we find our lives except that way?

> *The moon seems to be high over the mist
> now, for there is light everywhere out-
> side; so that, on peering into the night,
> it is with surprise all is found obscure
> and not easily definable or detachable
> amid the faint daze of light that feigns
> to illumine the valley. The women
> have become only black shapes upon
> the square litten patch which is the
> doorway surrounded by the blackness
> of the barn. A dog howls somewhere
> far away.*

LIB.
That dog sounds from some low-set roadside farm;
What does it hear?   *There is a short silence.*

MAUDLIN.   Women, what does it see?
They say dogs howl when someone's fetch goes
    by.

LIB.
Mayhap it is the husband-shapes a-coming.

MIDSUMMER EVE

NAN.
We shall see nought but what is in our thoughts.
Yet I'd be very fain to see my man
When Gib at Hornbeam-Shallows lost his wife
He had to hire a wench for the first time
And at next Martimas hiring came to me
And offered me four pounds for the half year,
Saying he'd give me his wife's milking coats
To make it up, ay, and her two best shawls,
One darned across the neck-place, one loom-new;
I told him I would liefer have her shoes—
That frightened him so well he stammered off.
But Sib had heard; she drew him with her eyes,
And said she'd go for three pounds and the shawls
If he would let her use a gown sometimes.
Then at each hiring she stayed on for less,
Till in the third year's end he wedded her;
And so she's gotten shawls and shoes as well.
I missed a savoury chance, for he is old
And childless; both stock and land are his:
Ay, if I had gone quietly to him
Ere now I might have had him for myself.

BET.
I should not wait three years for any man. . . .
When Sib would hire a lass Gib said his other
Had done without for seven and thirty years,
And he had ringed her but to save her wage:
At first he sent the hind to milk for her,
But stopped him soon, saying that men's hands
Made cow-teats horny; then at Whitsun hiring
He let him go, grutching it was waste
With such a goodly woman in the yard;
So now she has to herd and fork and winnow,
To drive the cart and take a side of thatch.

154

MIDSUMMER EVE

Gib says young wives are better worth their fodder
Than worn ones. Truly she has a gown sometimes,
For she goes ever in an old woman's wear—
He says the other's gear will last her days.
Nan must surely see more than that to-night.

LIB.
Ah, but Sib knows him: he does so fondle her;
He lets her hair down every eve to spread it
And feel the pleasure of the comb's sleek goings,
Bidding her " Stand over" as when a cow
Rubs up against the boust at milking-time;
While, when they gleaned their harvest fields by
　　moonlight
To stint the widows, he would bend down as she
Bobbed up a mouth all blackberry-stains to kiss...
Before she is fit for kitchen toil again
He will so wonder how she has grown the mis-
　　tress.　　　　　　　　　　　　BET *laughs.*

URSEL, *shivering.*
Hush, do not laugh; it creeps up in the roof,
And drips on us again like the thick water
Through the black pulpy thatch-leak in Novem-
　　ber
That laugh sounded as lonely as one flail
　　　　　　　　　　　　There is a silence.

MAUDLIN.
The heifer ceased to moan a moment past—
It seems as if it holds its breath to listen. . . .
　　　　　　　　　　　　There is a long silence.

BET.
I need to speak, but what I have forgotten. . . .

MIDSUMMER EVE

URSEL.
Lass, do not make us speak, or we may miss it. .

MAUDLIN.
O, do not speak to us, or we may miss it. . . .

LIB.
We could not hear you for this listening.

NAN.
I look so deeply that I cannot see
I cannot listen for it for listening. . . .

> *There is a long silence which pulses slowly
> with half-caught heavy breaths and
> slight restless rustlings of the hay in
> which the women seem motionless.*

BET.
Do I feel something? Do we feel something
growing? . . .

> *Quiet steps are heard to shift the lane's
> pebbles. The women look sharply at
> each other, start soundlessly to their
> feet and lean toward the door; they
> move forward half eagerly, yet each
> seeks to put the others before her, so
> that as they near the door* NAN *poises
> unwillingly foremost; when the light
> catches their faces they seem about to
> laugh.*

NAN.
Nay, I'll not meet it—perhaps it is not mine
I will not know aforetime to despoil
The gradual joy of waking to a man
I will not lose one feeling of dear change,

156

MIDSUMMER EVE

Or slur it by being conscious of the next.
Yet even then love should be marvellous
As the surprise of secret lights expected . . .
O, if I meet some one I do not want. . . .
Come, maids, join hands and let us go together—
Still, we might make too sure.

> *When* NAN *is across the threshold the
> others huddle back. The steps come
> nearer. In the road beyond* NAN *a
> woman appears quietly from the left;
> so far as it is possible to see, her
> features and array are the counter-
> part of* NAN'S.

NAN, *continuing.*   Hey, here's a woman . . .
Lib, did you tell the slatterns at Cherry-Close
    mill?
Nay, 'tis some rag-bag sleeper under hedges. . . .

BET, *in an undertone of wonder.*
Why are their coats alike?

NAN, *turning her head and calling.*
                        Ursel, Ursel,
She's from the farm—our granary has been
    searched;
For see, she wears my old plum petticoat—
Come, let us strip her and pen her in a sty . . .
But   I have on my old plum petticoat . . .
And how can she come from the farm when she
    goes to the farm?

LIB, *hastily and below her breath.*
Fetches and wraiths . . . fetches and wraiths
    fetches and wraiths . . .   *Peering about her.*
Is there no way from here?

157

MIDSUMMER EVE

MAUDLIN, *under her breath.*

My mother's grandmam
Saw her own fetch a week before she died. . . .

BET, *in a low tone.*
Come through the neat-house ere we too see
    ours—
Ursel, come . . . come. . . .

URSEL, *in a hushed voice.*

If all your days are used
Your fetch can meet you at the neat-house door—
Ah, stay, for Nan will need us when   . that
    goes. . . .
        BET, LIB, *and* MAUDLIN *hurry and crowd
        into the mistal unheedingly. Mean-
        while the woman has passed from left
        to right along the road, turning always
        to* NAN *and holding out her arms to
        her.*

NAN, *leaning out toward her with her hands pressed
    over her heart.*
Her unapparent features make me feel
How others must feel my face.   The droop of
    her skirt
Is creeping on my hips. . . . I have watched my
    feet
Draw sideways so. . . . Her shadow is long like
    mine
About the bosom . . . I wish I could touch her
    hair—
I know so well the tingle and smell of my hair . . .
Is this a fetch?
        She reaches forward as if she would follow,
158

until she is in the middle of the road;
the woman passes from sight to the
right. NAN's *body loosens; she turns*
confusedly to the barn and sees UR-
SEL's *face pale in the shade.*

NAN, *continuing.* O, Ursly, where have I gone?
I have lost myself, for I was here but now
        She remembers and shakes.
Dear soul, what did you see?

URSEL, *taking her in her arms.*
        I saw what you saw.

NAN.
Was it my fetch?

URSEL.   I think it was a fetch.

NAN, *numbly.*
I must be going to die. . . . I cannot feel so
There's nought I want to do when I am dead
      She is silent a moment, then seems
      startled into sobbing.
O, Ursel, Ursel, I cannot let me die. . . .

URSEL.
Folk say a fetch is seen at its departing
From a cold house whence it shall lead a soul;
But this comes like a child-birth closing in,
And so perchance it does but signify
The consciousness of death that breaks in all.
We stand outside the process of the earth
And watch it as immortals; and consider
Death, which we think a deeply moving thing
(Observing eagerly its fine emotions,

MIDSUMMER EVE

The impressive strangeness of its mean romance,
Its strong-tanged character and accidents,
And all the keen new chances it affords
For sympathy and for imagination),
But think not to connect it with ourselves—
So sure we are all 's possible to us.
Then a near comprehension that is love
Of trees or sheep, songs or some man or woman,
Shakes us one day and nothing is the same,
Because we grow aware that we must leave
The very joy that lights ourselves for us
And shows where we may greaten for its sake.
'Tis life's beginning; we perceive the earth
And go down into it and nestle to it
Defeatedly before its larger thought:
Numbly we measure ourselves by all we see,
We feel uneasily yet willingly
Each thing that happens may happen to us too,
And we are cheated by each grief unsuffered—
Yea, ever we interrogate decay
To know our own duration; we must touch
Each lovesome thing lest it or we should fade
Until the searching quiver of contact reaches
And makes us conscious where we can be love-
    some;
We find ourselves in others and thus learn
How others are in us, and so we creep
To large experiences we could not think—
Effectual perfection of ripe life;
The earth and all the darling ways of it
Are ours by love, for all that we must leave
Comes into us and makes us live it swiftly
Lest we should miss some thing. So that one love
Insists that every love in earth shall feed it,
To keep it from the unsafety of ignorance

And let our brief days yield their sweetness up.
Such is the consciousness of death—ah, such
Must be made yours; mayhap this is the way.

NAN.
The consciousness of death.   Though that be
    all,
It is too much: even if this fetch abides
Unnumbered years ere I see it depart,
Yet all is made unsure and I may sink
Before I have felt half I need to feel.
I must make every passion in myself,
Have each emotion of my wilful sowing—
The pain of sap, the pain of bud and bloom,
Of hard green fruit sun-bruised to thick gold juice,
The pain of the sharp kernel in the pulp
(Transmuter of sweet to inmost bitterness),
The pain of orderly corruption too—
Of the withdrawing sap, of the sick falling
Into long grass beneath the rain-soaked boughs,
Of gentle decomposing for small roots;
So that if death's the end, the true completion,
I could believe myself fulfilled and ripe,
A sufferer of the topmost joy and grief,
And past the need of any eternity
O, I desire old age, because old age
Has more capacity, more ways of joy. . . .

> *Her sobs hide her words.* URSEL *leads
> her to the hay and seats her among it
> again and herself by her, putting her
> arms about her and drawing her head
> down upon her bosom.*

URSEL.
Old age must sit and wait as we must wait

MIDSUMMER EVE

We can grow old so quickly in our souls
One utters a love-call and no answer comes,
One suffers motherhood within one's heart
Of cold unconscious children who can render
A tolerance of affection more remote
Than strait denial; and such maternity
Waits not for any bearing through the body
When love has come maternity must follow,
And if the body may not be made fruitful
The spirit chooses its own fruitfulness:
All that we miss is happening in others,
Others are feeling all we yearn to feel,
And if we will not let ourselves forget
How love has wrung us we pass through it with
    them. . . .
Ah, wonder, joy, of contact that enlarges
Our bodies' possibilities and times,
And gathers life for us to nourish
          A stifled cry from BET *is heard from the*
          neat-house.

BET.   Aa—h. . . .

NAN, *sinking back faintly in* URSEL'S *arms.*
Does   it return and . . . call?

URSEL.   Hush, 'tis Bet's voice. . . .
          After a brief interval filled with slight
          sounds, BET *appears in the neat-house*
          doorway; she peeps before her until
          she sees the two women in the hay.

BET, *in a low eager tone.*
Ursel, Ursel.
              URSEL *rises and goes toward her.*
      The cow has died   in the dark.

MIDSUMMER EVE

When I returned but now by the yard door
I missed the boust and groped into her stall—
And did not know until I heaved and spread
Up a flat softness that went sick beneath me
With long stiff shakings, while her unearned wind
Broke far within, then slid against my cheek . . .
I could have borne it if she had been cold;
But she was nearly cold, so that I felt
A thread-thin warmth I could not stay nor make...

NAN, *approaching* BET *swiftly from behind and
grasping her shoulder.*
Is the cow dead?

BET, *shrinking from her touch.*
                Nannie, the cow is dead.

NAN.
I milked her last of all, and now my fetch
Has milked her too; will . . . it . . . take all from
     me
I own through love?
(*To* BET.)   Why did you shrink from me?

BET.
I did not shrink from you; what need is there?
      NAN *holds out her arms to her; again she
        draws away from* NAN.
Nannie, I cannot help it. . I cannot help it. . . .
There's more than this world in you, and I know
     not
What you might do to me past your own will:
You have seen your fetch and are not one of us,
For we know not your being's dim half-con-
     ditions . . .
And maybe if you touch ought that has life
163

You make it that your fetch can take it too—
So died the heifer. . . . Or maybe your least touch
Draws life from others to win you a few hours;
Or you are of the dead, and call folk to them
Through sympathy of the senses' understand-
ing.
Poor Nannie . . . O, poor Nannie . . . O, poor
Nannie.

> *She sobs loudly, stooping to wipe her eyes
> with her petticoat-hem.*

URSEL, *while seeking to still her.*
Let us turn home to bed: we shall not sleep;
But once we're stripped we can relax our bodies,
Lying past thought for misery till insight
Returns again and brings us the proportion
Of all   and us. . . .

NAN.   I shall bide here till dawn
To see if . . . I return and go out . . . out . . .
    (*To* BET.)
Have you left Lib and Maudlin hiding some-
    where;
Or do they home by now?

BET, *overcoming her tears gradually.*
                    We fled from here
When . . . when . . . and reached the neat-yard
    ere we knew;
We climbed the knoll and passed behind the barn;
Then through the corn land, dew-wet to our hearts,
We beat the thick rye down that choked our feet
Amid its shaggy sighing stilly weight,
Until the cottages at Damson-Closes
Hung o'er us like a dark broody-winged hen—

MIDSUMMER EVE

We shunned the watcher's light where the old
    woman
Waits for her death, and dripped into the lane
Soft as cast shadows.   Ever all feared to speak:
Yet I went with the others through lost fields,
Straining to see the thing we prayed to miss,
Because I knew I dared not near the homestead;
Until I felt that neither should I dare
A more remote returning by myself—
When, loitering unnoticed by those trances,
I sought even you rather than be alone.

NAN, *rigidly, her head having been long averted
    to the barn's doorway.*
I hear my feet.

URSEL, *in alarm.* Nan, do not go. . . .

NAN.   I must.

BET, *wildly.*
Again. . . . Wherever shall I go alone?
> *She tugs her cap-strings loose and her cap
> over her eyes; she breathes so deeply
> that her trembling is heard by her
> breath as she fumbles her way into
> the mistal. The quiet steps are heard
> again; as* NAN *approaches the thres-
> hold the woman reappears to the right
> and passes down the lane to the left,
> always holding out her arms to* NAN,
> *whose arms hang tensely at her sides
> while her fingers twitch at her petti-
> coat as she holds back and back from
> meeting the embrace.* URSEL *tries to
> go to* NAN, *but she cannot trail her*

feet after her nor draw down her hands
that cover her face.

NAN.
How have I parted? . . . Where am I in deed? . . .
What of me is unseen? . . . . . . Go.

The woman having disappeared to the left,
still opening her arms to NAN, NAN
turns and totters to the door's edge on
that side; thence she feels her way
supportedly along the door, but when
she comes to its end she slides to her
knees; after moving a little farther so,
she sinks forward on her face and
crawls blindly toward URSEL'S *feet.*
At the fall URSEL'S *hands drop; she*
reaches to NAN, *kneels by her, feels*
her heart and hands, holds her own
hand before NAN'S *mouth and nos-*
trils; then with one swift movement
she loosens her own raiment nearly to
her waist, and, lying against NAN,
clasps her in her arms and gathers
her into her bosom.

URSEL.   Nan. . . . O, Nan. . . .
The two lie quite still; the stirred dust
settles on them slowly and greyly in
the moonlight.

CURTAIN.

LAODICE AND DANAË

" And, O, perchance it is the fairest lot
At once to be a queen and be forgot;
For queens are oft remembered by the weighed
Wild dusky peacock-flashing sins they played,
But queens clean-hearted leave us and grow less,
Lost in the common light of righteousness."

From KING RENÉ'S HONEYMOON: A
MASQUE, Scene vii.

TO B. J. FLETCHER

O RARE Ben Fletcher, oft I bless
Your rotund Jacobean name;
If the great crew could still express
Their hearts in their dim place of Fame,
As once at Globe or Mermaid-ales,
With love your liking they would greet
For country things and queens' mad tales
And lines with sounding feet.

But in this troublous newer time
Such fellows have not filled your days,
So it is left for me to chime
These quieter verses of your praise:
For a fair theme I need not strive
While manhood knows as boyhood knew
The joys of art, the joys of life,
I have received from you.

What days could ever be so long
As those our pristine Summers poised
O'er a charmed valley isled among
Their bright slow-breaking tides unnoised?
Then Dials were new and came to stir
A passionate thirst within the eyes;
Each dawn was a discoverer
Of poets unearthly wise.

First-comer of my friends, the years
Behold much friendship fade and set ·
The shrunken world imparts its fears,
Most men their early power forget.
But art stays true for us, and we
In it are steadfast: for a sign
Its wonder joins us changelessly
Your name stands here with mine.

March 8th, 1909.

ARGUMENT

Antiochus *Theos*, one of the Hellenic Kings of the East of the line of Seleucus, reigned in Antioch. He had espoused Laodice his kinswoman, according to the usage of his race; but after many years he put her from him, and took to wife Berenice, daughter and sister of Ptolemys of Egypt, for reasons of state.

Laodice withdrew to Ephesus and kept court there: long affection, resurgent, sent Antiochus thither to join her. Shortly afterward he died at Ephesus in Laodice's care.

Berenice and Laodice then warred, each to gain the kingdom for her child: the infant son of Berenice disappeared, and eventually Seleucus II., the son of Laodice, held the throne of Antiochus.

In the course of their wars Laodice retired from Ephesus on finding that Sophron, the governor of the city, secretly trafficked with the party of Berenice. While she sat in some adjacent city Sophron unsuspiciously rejoined her counsels; she immediately devised his death, but he, being warned by his old love Danaé, the queen's favourite, saved himself by flight.

PERSONS:

LAODICE, a Queen of the Seleucid House in Asia.

DANAE, MYSTA, RHODOGUNE, BARSINE, and other Waiting-Women.

Three Women-Musicians.

SOPHRON, Seleucid Governor of Ephesus.

In Smyrna. B.C. 246.

LAODICE AND DANAË

Behind the curtain a woman sings to the accom-
paniment of a harp and a bell.

I WILL sing of the women who have borne
      rule,
The severe, the swift, the beautiful ·
I will praise their loftiness of mind
That made them too wise to be true or kind;
I will sing of their calm injustice loved
For the pride it fed and the power it proved.

Once in Egypt a girl was queen
Ashamed that her womanhood should be seen;
She wore a beard, she called herself king,
She was uneasy with governing;
She believed a king was greater than she,
So she found a king and his mastery.

In Smyrna sits a queen to-night
Who does not shine by another's light;
She has laid her husband on time's dust-heap,
But for that she holds not her title cheap;
New radiance comes on woman by her,
New force in woman is seen to stir.

She has taken the land and the sea from men;
She has shewn men the power of their source
      again. . . .

LAODICE AND DANAË

The curtain rises.

A lofty chamber of mingled Hellenic and Asiatic architecture is seen. The walls are of black stone: on the right a portal toward the front of the stage is concealed by a curtain embroidered with parrots and Babylonian branch-work; high and toward the back is a double window, with open cedar lattices, of an inner room: high in the opposed wall is a short arcade with a projecting gallery. An open colonnade extends across the rear wall at two-thirds of its height; its pillars support the roof: the platform of this colonnade is accessible by an open stair recessed in the wall.

QUEEN LAODICE reclines on a great divan set toward the left centre of the chamber. The musicians whose singing and playing have just ceased kneel on a Persian carpet before her: between them and the portal stands a tall brazier whence a wavering heat rises. A golden evening sky is visible through the colonnade, where DANAË leans against a pillar.

LAODICE.

BE silent now; I let you sing too much.
  I am awaiting now too many things
To bear this fret of waiting till you end
And I can think again. Be quietly gone.

The women go out.

DANAË.
You bade them sing to make one moment brief.

LAODICE.
What are you watching like a larger cat,

172

LAODICE AND DANAË

Sweetheart, little heart, noiseless and alert?
You shall not watch me like a prim wise cat.

DANAË.
I watch a girl sway slightly, near the tide,
As if rehearsing dance-steps in her heart;
She hangs lit snakes of sea-weed down her bosom;
She takes a letter from her bunchy hair. . . .
> *She laughs and leans over, holding the pillar.*

LAODICE.
Find me a ship, ships; dark ones, strange ones.
I must have ships, so find them, little heart;
And, more than all, a ship of Antioch.

DANAË.
How tiny a girl looks under these deep rocks. . . .
> LAODICE *yawns.*

Madam, I have searched well; yet until now
No deep-sea ship has passed the promontory;
Now a great ship with tawny sails comes on,
An ocean-threatening centaur for its prow.

LAODICE.
That is from Ephesus, not Antioch.
I purge one thought thereby and make repayment.
I am taken with an inward shivering:
Perhaps I am cold with night—come down and warm me.
> DANAË *descends and reclines by* LAODICE.

Haughty and passive and obedient,
May not my queen's bosom receive your head?
When I worked empery in Ephesus
That Sophron, governor—did he not love you?

LAODICE AND DANAË

DANAË
He said he did.

LAODICE.   And you?

DANAË.   I said he did.
Thereon he made too sure of me too soon:
It is unwise to let men be too sure,
And for that reason I hung up my silks
On a swart Nabatæan, having smeared her
With my rare private unguent, and concealed
     her
In his choice corner—where she bit his lip,
Then let her laughing teeth take light of moon.
There was no more of Sophron afterward.
Although I looked at him almost penitently. . . .

LAODICE.
No more? Was there no more, my little one?

DANAË.
Ah, yes. .   When he would never look at me
I felt I could not live outside his arms.
I went to him at night in a slave's skirt,
And by humiliating actions soothed
His wincing mind, until he stooped to me.
I had him soon. And then I tired of him.

LAODICE.
And then, indeed, there was no more at all?

DANAË.
I have not seen him since. We left that city.
You have my faith. You know I am all yours.

LAODICE AND DANAË

LAODICE.
That is quite well. He has no years for you;
He is found treasonous, and must be undone.
O, he goes out. . . . Dear, I am very cold.
Is it because my heart is cold? Men say it.

DANAË.
Your heart is warm to me.

LAODICE.   What do men say?

DANAË.
They say you fled to Sardis and to Smyrna
Because you poisoned him at Ephesus
And heard his feet when a room echoed.

LAODICE.   Him ?

DANAË.
Antiochus the God, your king and spouse.

LAODICE.
Why do they so consider me the cause?

DANAË.
You hold the physician Smerdis in more favour.

LAODICE.
And did I poison him, my Danaë?

DANAË.
Dear lady, surely.

LAODICE.   Surely.   It is sure.
Was I not made the Sister, natural wife?

LAODICE AND DANAË

Did he not change me for a daughter of Egypt
Robed with a satrapy, crowned by an isle?
She laved her body daily in Nile water,
Which can make fruitful even stones and virgins;
It soon brought forth the mud's accustomed spawn,
A valuable heir of all the lands.
How could she keep him? Needing me he
    turned:
Was it not best for him to die still needing me
And leave the amount of kingdoms to my boy,
The climbing vine of gold up Shushan's front,
The cedar palaces of Ecbatana,
Though Berenice sits in Antioch
Safe with her suckling, in her suckling's name?
Winds, bring to me a ship from Antioch.
Since that dread night when Mysta stept not down
With all you speechless ones to disarray me,
Have you not dreamed that I did poison her?
Her love is more than yours, for she had crept
To Antioch to sell herself in bondage
Where Berenice buys, that she may nurse
The child for Berenice—and for me,
While uncle Egypt plucks my crown for it.

DANAË.
Which fingers mixed the poison? See, I kiss
    them,
Trust them ever to do their will with me.
There is no poison in a poppy-seed;
The seedling draws its venom from the earth—
'Tis the earth's natural need for such event.

LAODICE.
Ay, but the disposition is in the seed;
I poison by a motion of the heart.

LAODICE AND DANAË

RHODOGUNE, *a Parthian waiting-woman,*
enters.

RHODOGUNE.
Madam, the governor of Ephesus
Comes newly from the harbour to your will.

DANAË.
Sophron!

LAODICE.   Lie still.   *A silence.*

RHODOGUNE.   Madam, must I go down?

LAODICE.
Bid this Ephesian governor to me.
          RHODOGUNE *goes out.* LAODICE *lays a*
          hand on DANAË'S *heart.*
          It is now twilight. SOPHRON *enters.*

SOPHRON.
Queen, am I swift enough to your commanding?

LAODICE.
I am ever rich in your discerning service.
Why came you by the sea?
          She sees that SOPHRON'S *gaze is fixed on*
          DANAË, *who does not look at him.*
                    Girl, stand behind me.
                    DANAË *obeys.*
Why came you by the sea?

SOPHRON.   Lady   the sea?

LAODICE.
Does not the way by land still fit mine urgence?

SOPHRON.
Your safety's urgence made it seem most good
To search the straits for masts of Ptolemy.

LAODICE.
Ha. . . . Yes. . . . And did you speak with any
   such?
             DANAË *looks at* SOPHRON *and shakes her*
             head.

SOPHRON.
The seas were void of alien keels to-night.

LAODICE.
Are there Egyptians seen in Ephesus?

SOPHRON.
None since the aged men who mummied the
   king.

LAODICE.
Tell me the common talk of Egypt's plan;
And what device to handle Ptolemy
Is in your friendly mind.

SOPHRON.
There 's but a common fear of Egypt's secret.
We cannot meet him yet unless the cities,
Yes, all these cities of men, take hands with us.

LAODICE.
Must I keep house in Smyrna still, my man?
Play queen in a corner harmlessly?

SOPHRON.   Madam,
The coast is safer here than at Ephesus,
Retreat on Sardis safer and more ready.

LAODICE AND DANAË

LAODICE.
I more withdrawn apart from my main kingdom,
Baffled from drainage of the unended East.
I have required you here because a word,
Perhaps a word malicious, has crept here:
It has been said that some Ephesian men
Have bartered for my town with Ptolemy—
Do you know any of these? Do they live?

SOPHRON.
There are none known: such could not sell past
    me.

LAODICE.
They use my palace: examine those about you.

SOPHRON.
There is no need: I know them to be clean.
       DANAË *again shakes her head, but more*
       eagerly.

LAODICE, *turning her head and looking up at*
    DANAË *suddenly.*
Why do you tremble, girl? There's nought to
    fear.
       As she begins to speak DANAË'S *hair is*
       shaken loose; a rose falls from it
       and breaks on LAODICE'S *shoulder.*
       LAODICE *laughs and plays with the*
       petals, continuing without pause.

LAODICE.
Do you drop me a sleepy kiss, maiden, my rare
    one?
But, O, you have so tumbled your hair to cull it—
Come hither, kneel, and I will bind it up.

LAODICE AND DANAË

DANAË, *obeying.*
Lady, I coiled it carelessly.   . Indeed
Such ministration is my precious pardon.

LAODICE.
Silk, silky silk so delicious to finger. . . .
Rose I held; ruby-glows; then dark hair in my
    hands.
Nay, I am hot; I burn; stay there and fan me.
Dear, do not cease at all.
                To SOPHRON.
                  Well, my captain?

SOPHRON.
You shall have men's minds searched in Ephesus.

LAODICE.
I like your mind. Also, I have considered
You must shut up your port, let out no ship;
Then Ptolemy shall be more sure each night
That he has wiped the seas   . till you slip out.

SOPHRON, *in stupefaction.*
Slip   out?

LAODICE.
           Ay, Sophron, fall on him.

SOPHRON, *eagerly.*   Yes, yes:
These things shall be, and you shall not complain.

LAODICE.
Nay, go not now; be my great guest this night.
The tide will take you not until more day,
And in the dawn, white hour of clearest thought,

LAODICE AND DANAË

I need more counsel from you for my deeds.
> *She claps her hands: Barsine, a Persian,*
> *enters.*

Let this strong captain be well feasted now
In winy webs of my embroidering—
Or—no—a purple suits his temper best;
And send a slave to him for him to rule.

SOPHRON.
Graciousness, yours: let me but stay my seamen.

LAODICE.
Haretas the Pisidian shall go down
Into the place of ships, but not my guest:
Entrust your ring to this, and she will bear it.
> BARSINE *and* SOPHRON *go out.* LAODICE
> *nods to herself.*

I saw his ring: it was a new green scarab.
> DANAË *ceases fanning without* LAODICE
> *heeding.*

RHODOGUNE, *outside.*
She-dog, come back and you shall have but whips.
> *A dirty woman runs in, bearing a bundle*
> *within her ragged robe;* RHODOGUNE
> *follows her*

LAODICE, *slowly.*
I have not need of rinds and lees to-night;
Come, take these out and burn them.

THE WOMAN.   Ay, come.

LAODICE, *starting up.*
Mysta, MYSTA, my joy! What have you there?

181

LAODICE AND DANAË

The thing a mother called Antiochus?

To RHODOGUNE.

Do you not know your fellow and my hand?

RHODOGUNE *retires.*

MYSTA.

I was the handmaid of a displaced queen;
I am dry nurse to the undoubted queen,
Come back merely to boast and make display
How lusty a baby grows in careful hands,
How noble I to carry a living king.

LAODICE, *leaping to her.*
Unwind, dishevel, give it up to me.

Clapping her hands.

Let there be lights above: I must see closely.
If I embrace you I shall touch it too.

*A woman hangs a lamp from long chains
over the gallery on the left, then with-
draws. After a moment she passes
along the colonnade from left to right
and disappears. A moment later she
leans from the latticed windows on
the right to light two lamps suspended
from the roof to a point immediately
below her. The lights are such that,
when the twilight has gone, the figures
of the persons are more definite than
their features, and the upper part of
the chamber is almost unlit. In the
meantime* MYSTA *has continued.*

MYSTA.
Nay, we are but harbour-drift from Antioch:
Come, take us out and burn us.

LAODICE AND DANAË

LAODICE.   Aha, Mysta.

MYSTA.
Touch not my hair; 'tis foul from many ships.

LAODICE.
I have ached by watching ships that were not
    yours.
Were you in Sophron's vessel? Did he know?

MYSTA.
She did not trust me soon to tend her child,
Returning oft like the uneasy cat:
When I had slipt these rags on it and me
I herded with night-women by the shore.
Ere there, I passed a rift in palaces,
Moment of empty street and Berenice
Marching with hunger in her bright fixed eyes,
Champing her golden chain—one hand on it
Tugged her mouth downward—one hand smote
    a spear
Upon the stones as she stepped on and on
Toward the house of Cæneus your known friend.
They spied the harbour; I must leave by land;
Then was some tale of fishers, trading sloops:
Sophron knows not the thief like a fierce mother
Whose hard feet last left ship at Ephesus—
Where Ptolemy is looked for eagerly.
> *As she speaks* LAODICE *has drawn a
> scarf from her shoulders, twisted it
> and strained it in her hands; it tears
> and she throws it down.*
> MYSTA *holds out the child to her.*
'Twas warm and quiet so long. Let it live.

183

LAODICE AND DANAË

LAODICE, *taking the child and scanning it.*
Let me read here:
This is the mould, wrongly retouched and spent—
It is his child and yet I have not known it
                              Clasping it closely to her.
I am the changeless mother of this race,
And this a younger seed. By the opened womb
I have decided being: and I decide.
Much Asia has been spanned to leave it here,
More Asia will be narrowed by her searchers;
Mysta might die next time. It must die.
I reached my hand and took it to make sure
My order and number of children still were true.
I have looked on it—its purport is completed.

MYSTA.
It could be hid for ever: let it live.

LAODICE.
Mysta shall need my ritual bath and wardrobe;
Serve me by delicate sleep. Mysta must go.
            She kisses MYSTA *and leads her to the
                 portal.* MYSTA *goes out passively.*

LAODICE.
Danaë, pile me cushions and hollow them—
There in the shadowed seat beyond the breeze.
No; larger cushions with no rough gold in
    stitchings.
One softer for his head—now hold it there
Till I can kneel and lay him in the dimmest,
For he may sleep a little yet. Ay, so.
I had well-nigh forgotten to appoint
Sophron a chamber.

LAODICE AND DANAË

DANAË.   Madam, I will go.

LAODICE.
You speak too loudly. Madam, you will remain:
I need you to cast gums upon the censer
To make me drowsy—I must sleep some mo-
    ments.

DANAË.
Storax alone, or juniper?

LAODICE.   O, storax.
            DANAË *goes to a recess in the wall near
            the portal, and takes out a painted
            bowl. She pours grains from it slowly
            upon the brazier; brief cloudy flames
            illumine her face.*
Did the Silk-People shape that bowl?

DANAË.   Maybe. . . .
I could burn up the world like this to-night,
To make an end of conflicts and of burdens.
            As LAODICE *claps her hands* BARSINE
            hurries in breathlessly.

BARSINE.
Queen, Queen.

LAODICE, *watching* DANAË.
            Make ready fragrantly and freshly
Chamber for Sophron next to that of Smerdis.
Then send Smerdis with knives and drugs to me.
            DANAË *opens her mouth as if to speak—
            the flames fall as she holds the bowl
            poised motionlessly.*

LAODICE AND DANAË

BARSINE.
Sophron—none can find him; he has gone.
>DANAË *lets the contents of the bowl slide
>into the brazier; a shaft of flame
>flares high, she averts her face.*

LAODICE.
Ho, are we dropping roses all the time?
Men; bring me men and torches and sharp
    spears—
A boat to cut the Centaur's rudder-ropes
I will go down and take him back . . . Hui
>*She sweeps out followed by* BARSINE.

DANAË.
O, Sophron, out by the land! Nay, he knows
    more—
And she, and she; watch-towers divide this earth,
Horses go here; and he may save a ship.
>*She draws aside the curtain to look beyond.*
May women's skirts impede you, ravening queen.
>*She ascends swiftly to the colonnade: a
>starry night shows her form dimly.*
Fishers' small lights, be drenched—you show too
    much
At height of settling gulls above the water
Ah . . . h, nothing, nothing. Something will
    not happen,
And let this life go on again. Nothing.
Yet . . . yet . . . the air is beating on my temples
As though a rabble murmured beyond hearing.
>RHODOGUNE *enters.*

RHODOGUNE.
Danaë, are you here?

186

LAODICE AND DANAË

DANAË.   I am here.

RHODOGUNE.
Where is the Queen?

DANAË.   Nearing the shore by now.

RHODOGUNE.
I have a drunken woman with nine snakes
That follow her as freshets a drowned body,
Then lift wise sibilant heads in guardian swaying;
Her lair could well be traced by emptied streets.
She is too drunk to speak, but sings the better
A praise of poisonous snakes and the fools of wine,
While in the night they circle and streak for
          answer
Like wine-cups' lines of light, black rubies' gleams.
Shall I not bring her for the Queen to use,
Who loves delights like dangers come too near?

DANAË.
Put her away in a safe place till morning—
The Queen is smouldering again to-night,
And, if she sees your epileptic mummer,
Will make us tie her up with her own serpents. . . .
Babble no more to me—I must be watching.

RHODOGUNE.
You are not the Queen, although the Queen's
          plaything;
Deign not your high commandments unto us.
                              She goes out.

DANAË.
Sophron, your bare grand neck's a tawny pillar

LAODICE AND DANAË

To lean a cheek against in burning noons;
Your careless eyes look deeplier than you know;
You must be kept in life. . . . Down there, down
    there
Is something darker, swifter than the sea
An unseen smoky glare is mirrored now.
That was his boat: he is gone. . . . Sophron,
    Sophron!
The sea is suddenly empty—and all places.
I have given him to mine enemies. She'll not
    kill him.
Now I must waken and repent my dreams:
Ay, Sophron, get you gone—I am whole again;
I am the Queen's—and O, farewell, farewell.
             She descends the stair slowly.
I am the Queen's indeed. Is she yet mine?
Ditizele—
A VOICE, *from within the cedar lattice.*
        Who is it calls me?

DANAË.   Danaë.

THE VOICE.   Yes?

DANAË.
The queen has spoilt my rose—throw me a young
    one.
       A rosebud falls from the lattice: DANAË
        sets it in her hair.
Thanks, dear. . . . She has put up my hair awry—
It will remind her she put up my hair.
       She shakes down her hair and knots it
        again, holding the rose-stalk in her
        mouth until she can replace it.
These Asiatic nights ruin the hair,

LAODICE AND DANAË

Their humid heat puts out its inner lights—
Mine waves with gleams no more than manes of
    Irân
Now she has left the shore—now she will set
Her feet upon the stairs like setting of teeth. . . .
       The child cries a little once: DANAË *goes*
          to it.
O, baby, the old silence of palaces
Is settling on you steadily. Your crying
Is shut within—and shall be farther enclosed.
One light small cry shows all so much too quiet.

LAODICE, *who has entered noiselessly and come*
    close behind DANAË.
Ay, do you consort with mine enemies?

DANAË, *wailing.*
Ah .   Ah . . . I sickened with the secret thing
The too faint sound that crept about my neck.

LAODICE, *slipping an arm about her.*
Nay, Rose-Locks, calm thy heart; I did but tease
Thy mothering this lost child, kings' waif and
    surplus.
Rare nurses his: the next will be the last:
Some treachery will ever draw toward him.
Rest you again upon the Persian couch,
And I will sit with you and eomfort you.
          Leading her to the divan.
Do not forget the cherishing of a queen:
I could not catch your Sophron for you, child.

DANAË.
I did not want him: he is better gone.
189

LAODICE AND DANAË

LAODICE.
Yet such delight to lead him to your arms:
You said you looked at him almost penitently.

DANAË.
Madam, you mock me; I have passed from him.

LAODICE.
Yes, yes; but rapture, for your mind severe,
Lies in the nearness of wise and powerful men—
As once for famous high Leontion,
That philosophic courtesan your mother.
Let be; but tell me of his quietest scheme.

DANAE.
I know him not: I never knew his mind.
> *Several women appear dimly at the latticed
> windows and the gallery.*

LAODICE.
Ah, well . . . I am tired, and it is your dear turn
To open your arms. Hold me and I will nestle,
Will murmur for you to hear along your neck.
What shall we do to-morrow, Danaë?

DANAË.
Fair mistress, I can dance for you to-morrow.

LAODICE.
Yes, but my dainty cannot dance all day—
She must have long, long quiet for her thoughts.

DANAË.
Then shall I wing the bright and silken birds
About the border of your Persian mantle?

LAODICE AND DANAË

LAODICE.
How should I do without you so many hours?

DANAË.
Your Parthian has a witch of snakes for you—

LAODICE.
I can charm snakes and even pith their fangs.

DANAË.
This is a rare one and, if she is drunken,
Does uncouth things delicious to the senses.
Steep in her wine the herb that makes insane—

LAODICE.
The herb. . . .?

DANAË.
   The viscous plant that grows i' your chamber:
Strange longer serpents shall be swiftly snared
And mixt untamed with hers, for you to read
Her gaping and ridiculous tragedy
As the cold perils sober her to pallor.

LAODICE.
It is not novel: with a secret call
I have turned snakes upon such things before.
I am learned and I need some graver pang
Something as unsuspected as to tell you
That I had poisoned you three hours ago,
And see you disbelieve—begin to believe.

DANAË.
But you did not.

LAODICE AND DANAË

LAODICE.   There is the disbelief.
A pause.

If I had done so I should here avouch
I could not do it—then await a sign.

DANAË.
Ah, I am yours. . . . You have not doomed me yet.
Queen with the wells of night for human eyes,
Let us descend upon the sea to-morrow,
Rule your own kingdom by your cedarn barge:
We will recline together, hushed as here—
Save for the waters' converse just beneath,
Permeant as my pulse veiled by your cheek.

LAODICE.
I am uneasy now and should disturb you—
And thence your restlessness would chafe me
       more.
I must make sure that you will lie quite still:
May I so still you? Then you shall to sea.
We'll sail about the limit of the lands
Until you reach the river of Babylon.

DANAE.
So much in one rapt day?
The days of life can never compass that.

LAODICE.
Not in a day, but in a day and night:
Conceive the night, my Danaë, the night—
It is the natural state of being and space,
Briefly interrupted by casual suns.
Much unknown empires are attained in night—
Perhaps not Babylon, yet far enough.
One night can be a very proper length.

192

LAODICE AND DANAË

DANAË.
You mean that I am poisoned after all.

LAODICE.
Indeed, my Danaë, it is not so.
In this barbaric land, this bright harsh dye-pot,
Peopled by camels and cynocephali
And hairy men of soiled uncertain hue,
O, do you not remember nights of Athens
Built well about with marbles and clear skies,
Wherein your mother and such noble women
Conversed with poets and heroes in lit groves,
And life subtled? Have you not longed for them?
I am sending you to such a farther country,
Away from this shrunk mummy of live earth.

DANAË.
Madam, I know you not—when must I leave you?

LAODICE, *clapping her hands.*
It is the hour, and you shall launch to-night.
Women, women, come hither every woman.
> *The faces disappear from the upper
> windows: eleven women appear on
> the colonnade, some from each side,
> and descend the stair rapidly.*

Get to your knees about us—both knees.
Stand up, my Danaë, be overbearing.
Women, when any woman has a kingdom
And is a regnant being, does it not suit
That in the disposition of her state
Women should figure her and power afar?
This kingdom I control has thrones of cities,
So many that I, when I would sit therein,
Must cast my shadow there: and chief of these

LAODICE AND DANAË

Is Babylon the nest of bygone things.
'Tis to that Babylon I now appoint
My bosom's clasp, my Danaë, for satrap;
She shall oppress among dead queens and gods,
Keep house where sheer dominion walks, com-
    mand
Enamelled palaces with copper roofs,
Pillars with gardens for their pediments—
Staircase for Anakim in Babylon:
And when ye are as dear to me as she
Ye shall advance upon such larger ways.

DANAË.
O, what is this you do? I am lost in it.

A WOMAN.
But how? The duplicate queen holds Babylon.

LAODICE.
It shall be mine again ere Danaë's advent
Danaë, sister of pearls, do I displease you?

DANAE.
Tell out your purpose, though I wreck by it.

LAODICE.
Could higher estate persuade such disbelief?
Barsine, now disburden of its store
The old brass coffer in my inner house—
The gems, the flower-striped silks, the mousse-
    lines
Worn by such royal girls of Babylon;
So rare a satrap as we do devise
Must be as Babylonish as her earth.
                BARSINE *goes out.*

LAODICE AND DANAË

Put out your hand, young princess, dip your hand
Among these herded common indiscretions,
And gratefully they'll mouth it. Nay, I'll lead you.

SECOND WOMAN.
Madam, remember me when you are mighty.

THIRD WOMAN.
And, O, forget not me.

LAODICE.
Arise, you humbled ones, jealous too long;
Take off her Greekish marks of my poor service,
Make ready her precious body to be tangled
In clotted skeins of her affiliate province.
> *The women strip* DANAË *of all but her*
> *under-robe.*
O friend, I do reproach you, for your gay heart
Has surely turned from me too easily
When something in you fades and alters so . . .
I have done this—my cherished, still keep mine . . .
> BARSINE *enters, her arms heaped with*
> *robes*: LAODICE *fingers them.*
These are your pretties. Greeks know not how to
    use
Layers of denial—you Persian, can you say?

BARSINE, *attiring* DANAË *in the new garments.*
These silken trousers tied above the knees,
Yet falling to the feet, are first.

LAODICE.   Ay, so.

BARSINE.
And now this inner gown shrinks close.

LAODICE AND DANAË

LAODICE.   Ay, so.

BARSINE.
Then this brocady robe with fan-flung train
And widening muffling sleeves.

LAODICE, *holding up a sleeve.*   Can it be so?
Pure Greeks conceive not slavery of sleeves.

BARSINE.
The pointed citron shoes.

LAODICE.   Not even sandals?

BARSINE.
There needs a shawl like gardens for a girdle,
But none was hoarded.

LAODICE.   Put your own on her.
Give me the jewels: I wish to play with the
     jewels.

BARSINE.
In the horn sphere: press on the metal hands.
The strings of golden tears and yellow stones
Hang hidy in the hair. I will unbind
Your lady's locks and shew you.

LAODICE.   Keep off: I must unloose them,
It is my custom.

DANAË, *in a low voice.*   O what are you doing?

BARSINE.
Round to the temples, so: this drops upon the
     brow

LAODICE AND DANAË

That breast of gold—pierced roses, diamond
    dew—
Curves on the head, no heavier than your hand . . .
Coils chime upon the ankles—the East walks
    slowly

LAODICE.
We come to the necklace.

BARSINE.   Yes, but it is lacking.

LAODICE, *to the* SECOND WOMAN.
You white-faced marvel, body of straight lines,
Give me your necklace dropt inside your chiton.

SECOND WOMAN.
O, do you see it? I cannot let it go—
It was my sister's, and she is dead since.
    Ah . . h

LAODICE, *snatching the necklace roughly.*
'Tis well for you it did not strangle you
When caught: but ye are all so envious yet.
There, Danaë, my hands shall finish you.
A painted wonder this I have created—
I am no better than the rest before it,
And I will do my homage, knees and lips.

DANAË, *faintly.*
What is the end, ah me!

LAODICE.   But in true Asia
Great ladies must live veiled; they are too choice
For foreign casual sight.

BARSINE, *veiling* DANAË.   This is the veil.

197

LAODICE AND DANAË

LAODICE, *peeping behind the veil.*
Bound so beneath the eyes? Show slipper-tips?
Indeed you are ended, Danaë, and shall part.
Farewell! Farewell! Fare delicately! Fare
    swiftly!
Will you go down by Ephesus, my rose;
Or all the sea?

FIRST WOMAN. Not Babylon by sea!

LAODICE.
If not to Babylon, yet far enough.
Tie up these arms and bind these feet together;
Bear to the columns and cast her forth to sea,
Where she shall be my satrap of the darkness.
She has been dying many moments now,
She shall have burial as one who ceases
In a strange ship, unfriended on the deeps.
                    The women laugh.

FIRST WOMAN.
Joy—but wherewith, O Light?

LAODICE.   Your sandal-thongs:
You are good enough to obey me on bare feet.
    Several of the women hastily untie their
       sandals.

FOURTH WOMAN, *kneeling to bind* DANAË'S *feet.*
Forget not me to heel, my mighty lady.

VARIOUS WOMEN, *clustering about* DANAË *and*
    seizing her.
Come on, come on to Babylon, dread Madam....
Up and down to Babylon, cold Highness. . . .
I'll be her coiffing slave and tend her head. . . .

I'll be her nurse and hold her in my breast.
More humbly I will take her feet in mine.
What honour to be trusted with such life—
A priceless load. . . . Ah, do not let it fall.

DANAË, *to* LAODICE.
Yet I have served you well.

LAODICE.   Yea, very well.
Whereto did Sophron flee?

DANAË.   I do not know.

LAODICE.
Tell me why Sophron fled, and what he knew.
                                   A pause.
Tell even where your thoughts are following him.
                                   A pause.
Even at what point of my research in him
Your heart lifted, and I will keep you back.
                                   A pause.
Then are you both completed and concluded.
Knot elbows too, and lift her to the columns.

DANAË.
Yet I have loved you.

LAODICE.
You are not mine: this earth shall not contain
    you.
I could unmake the stars to ensure darkness,
To cheat me of the places that have known you.

DANAË.
Must I go out?

LAODICE AND DANAË

Then pay me for my spent devotion first.
Let not these spittly weeds close in and choke
    me;
Undrape these silk and Asiatic jeers;
Let me go loose, and I will go indeed
As far as your desire—serving you yet.

LAODICE, *severing* DANAE's *bonds with her dagger,
    then rending away her veil and upper gar-
    ments.*
Your rigid mortal bonds, .
Your isolating veil, . . .
Your scarf of earthly flowers,
Your robe that once was royal, .
Your chill, worn-out simarre,
Slide as the world slides.
Put off your useless shoes
To enter a holy place
Get to your high estate.

DANAË, *standing in her under-garment.*
Gather your jewels.

LAODICE.   You trifle to gain moments.

DANAE.
Give me one kiss.

LAODICE.   You have not time. These wait.
        Indicating the surrounding women.

DANAË.
Your house shall be the firmer by your sentence.
      *She takes the sleeping child in her arms,
      and mounts the stair quickly.*

LAODICE AND DANAË

SEVERAL WOMEN.
The child; she has the child.

LAODICE.   Yes. And then?

DANAË, *pausing by a column.*
The common run of men make small account
Of high religion; and they are very right.
I saved my lover, and I now receive
This recognition from the Powers who still
Dispose of us: Laodice killed hers,
And she is held deserving of all that honour.

LAODICE, *pointing at the* FOURTH WOMAN.
Thrust her down, you.
        DANAË *disappears while the* FOURTH
        WOMAN *stealthily mounts the stair.*
        LAODICE *has thrown herself on the*
        divan, with her back to the colonnade.
               To-morrow will be soon.
To-morrow I will sit with men in council,
And muster men to leaguer Ephesus.
These fretting hens, these women, burden me—
I know their eyes too well; let them keep hid.
To-morrow I will walk upon the harbour,
And board my ships and see them manned and
    ready—
No, no, I will not step toward the sea. .

SEVERAL WOMEN, *as* LAODICE *speaks.*
        Ai! Ai! Is she down? Not yet. .
I cannot see. . . . . No one can see.

SECOND WOMAN, *sobbing in the corner near the*
    stair.   My necklace!
Save my dear gems!

LAODICE AND DANAË

FOURTH WOMAN, *from the colonnade.*
> She is not here. She falls.

LAODICE.
Is that hoarse dashing how the surge receives
    her?

FOURTH WOMAN.
It is the old recession of the waves;
The rocks are bare. No movement could be seen;
No pallor could emerge. There is no sound.

LAODICE, *in a dull voice.*
She was as false as all the rest of you·
But she was brave. Remember that she died;
Be cowards still, and so be false and safe.
She had a lulling hand.   Put me to sleep.
> RHODOGUNE *goes toward her.*

CURTAIN

APPENDICES

APPENDIX A

" KING LEAR'S WIFE " was performed for the first time on 25 September 1915 at the Birmingham Repertory Theatre, with the following cast:

Lear	Mr. E. Ion Swinley.
Hygd . . .	Miss Cathleen Orford.
Goneril . . .	Miss Margaret Chatwin.
Cordeil . . .	Miss Betty Pinchard.
Merryn . . .	Miss Dorothy Taylor.
Gormflaith . . .	Miss Mary Merrall.
Physician . . .	Mr. Ivor Barnard.
Two Elderly Women	{ Miss Betty Pinchard. { Miss Maud Gill.

Costumes and decoration designed by Mr. Barry V. Jackson.

Production by Mr. John Drinkwater.

In the course of the production the song of the Elder Woman, toward the close of the play, was fitted with so appropriate a melody, by a fortunate modification of a folk-tune, that it seems well to continue the connexion by printing the arrangement here.

Rather quickly.

The louse made off un - hap-py and wet —A -

- humm, A-humm, A - hee— He's look-ing for us, the

A

lit-tle pet ; So haste, for her chin's to tie up yet, And

B   C

let us be gone with what we can get—Her ring for thee, her

gown for Bet, Her pock - et turned out for

✳   ✳ CODA.

me. .   me. .   .   .   .   .   .

This represents the extension of the melody used
for the final stanza of the song: it can be adapted to
the forms of the first and second stanzas by the omis-
sion of the sections A-C and B-C respectively. The
Coda is intended for use with the final stanza only.

————

APPENDICES

First performed in London on 19 May 1916 at His Majesty's Theatre, under the direction of Miss Viola Tree.

Lear	Mr. Murray Carrington.
Hygd	Lady Tree.
Goneril . . .	Miss Viola Tree.
Cordeil . . .	Miss Odette Goimbault.
Gormflaith . . .	Miss Julia James.
Merryn .	Miss Beatrice Wilson.
Physician .	Mr. H. A. Saintsbury.
Two Elderly Women	{Miss Ada King. {Miss Bertha Fordyce.

Play produced by Mr. John Drinkwater, and mounted by Mr. Purcell Jones: music by Mr. Ivor Novello.

SONGS
For the London performance of " King Lear's Wife."

I (p. 43)
Mother, it is my wedding morn;
Come, bring the linen fine,
And wash my face with milk so warm
Drawn from the young white kine.
The blackbird in the apple-tree
Was waking ere the day;
But I was ready sooner than he,
For I watched the night away.

II (p. 44)
The Queen has gone to bed
In the middle of the day;
But what about her bedfellow?
No one dares to say.

She cannot sleep at night:
She does not care to try;
The darkness makes her restless,
And nobody knows why.

APPENDICES

III (p. 48)

O, merry, merry will my heart be
When I can sit me down and rest:
If you would live to make old bones
Keep your knees off the kitchen-stones,
And go like a lady, warmly drest.

APPENDIX B

"THE CRIER BY NIGHT." was first performed by Mr. Stuart Walker's Portmanteau Theatre Company in Wyoming, U.S.A., in September 1916, and in New York at the Princess Theatre on 18 December 1916, with the following cast:

Hialti . . .	Mr. McKay Morris.
Thorgerd .	Miss Judith Lowry.
Blanid .	Miss Florence Buckton.
An Old, Strange Man	Mr. Edgar Stehli.

Play produced by Mr. Stuart Walker and mounted by Mr. W. J. Zimmerer.

SOME PRESS OPINIONS OF MR. BOTTOMLEY'S PLAYS

From "The Supernatural in Tragedy," by Professor C. E. Whitmore, Litt.D., of Harvard University, U.S.A. (Oxford University Press, 1915.) Pp. 315-317.

We have in the work of a very recent writer, Gordon Bottomley, a noteworthy attempt at the combination of Celtic and Northern feeling in a curious piece, "The Crier by Night," issued in 1902. . . . It owes a good deal to Mr. Bottomley's own imaginative power. The emotions of the play lie far from any ordinary circle of experience, and the characterization is of course very broad ; but the piece does convey its sense of a sinister power that preys on human lives, and is clothed in a style of grim but compelling beauty. Perhaps no more than an experiment, it is none the less individual and significant.

In a later and more achieved play, "The Riding to Lithend," 1909, we find Mr. Bottomley turning definitely to the North for his inspiration, and choosing a theme from the Njal-Saga. . . . A brief summary of course gives no idea of the march of the drama, which is remarkably compact and well-knit; but it serves to show the skill with which the ominous old women are introduced to heighten our sense of foreboding. In this play Mr. Bottomley is well on the road to an individual dramatic accomplishment, and it is a very encouraging symptom of the possible growth of a new branch of poetic tragedy.

From "New Voices : An Introduction to Contemporary Poetry," by Marguerite Wilkinson. (New York : The Macmillan Co., 1919.) P. 350.

Gordon Bottomley is one English poet who excels in the presentation of personality. In his dramatic poem, "King Lear's Wife," he gives us a totally new conception of the fabled king. . . . This poem is stark, uncompromising, grim . . . from beginning to end. But it is unforgettable. Each character is like a heroic statue rough-hewn from granite. . . . The expressions on the stone faces are cruel. But we have a sense of certainty as to the truth of it . . . it is a work of genius that the reader can never forget.

The late Edward Thomas in *The Daily Chronicle*, on "The Crier by Night."

The action of this one-act play takes place in a region where there are no mountains and no meres, in the gray chambers of a fantastic brain. It is a handful of dreams. No *ombres Chinoises* or "plays for marionettes" behind gauze were ever more unreal. And yet not unreal. For the poet and those readers whom he has a right to expect, these voices out of the mist are as real as Hamlet's or Paula Tanqueray's. . . . They are the more real because the poet's language and rhythm are true to the life of those beings that never lived, save in his fantasy. The dialogue is remarkably monosyllabic, and modulated with such infinite legitimate variations as make the blank verse perhaps the most delicate of our time . . . this patiently written little book is full of "natural magic" which will make a strong and enduring appeal to some.

The Outlook, in a middle article entitled "A Good Front Piece."

Here is real poetry. . . . The characterization is distinct, the impulse to sympathy is kept fluctuant from the pathetic Blanid to the rather stolid Hialti, and thence finally to the cruel Thorgerd. The workmanship is massive, elegant, clean. . . . Actor-managers in need of a curtain-raiser full of the fascination and the horripilation of exquisitely ghastly humanity and of exquisitely real poetry, will of course do worse than put on this piece at once. The ideal casts would include Mr. Martin Harvey as Hialti and Mr. Laurence Irving as the Crier. And Dr. Elgar would do well to write the music.

The Academy and Literature.

The book to which we would especially call attention is Mr. Gordon Bottomley's "The Crier by Night." It is in many ways a singular poem . . . there is in it a strong originality—originality in expression, originality even in conception . . . it is strangely impressive; one feels the sorcery. The poetry is sombrely strong, and has caught the spirit of Celtic legend with fidelity. . . . But no quotation will convey the power of

MR BOTTOMLEY'S PLAYS

the poem. Though its style catches something of the Celtic quality, its essential quality is darker, sterner, more grimly suggestive. A wild and morbid preternaturalism informs the brief drama, which certainly gives promise that Mr. Bottomley has it in him to work out a distictive vein of his own.

The Manchester Guardian.

Of earlier verse by Mr. Gordon Bottomley we said that it showed signs of talent and that something memorable might be looked for from its author . . . his one-act play in verse, "The Crier by Night," exhibits a headlong energy of imagination, some power of grasping elusive and baffling phases of deep feeling, a good deal of fertility in fresh and apt imagery, a good deal of the romantic gift for fixing on some strange, small, sensuous detail that touches a spring in the imagination of the reader, and makes him do the rest of a description for himself, and a good deal of the right sensitiveness to the precise sensuous quality of words themselves as sounds having an intrinsic interest and value, and not solely as definite symbols. . . No one who cares about poetry should, if he can help it, miss reading whatever Mr. Bottomley writes next it may well be something quite first-rate.

The Morning Post.

The character in "The Crier by Night" that most possesses one is Blanid. . . . Taken merely as a tale of mystery and terror it is very effective   Every page is eloquent of a high and delicate poetical temperament.

The Literary World.

We can honestly say that rarely have night-fall, harsh weather, and the supernatural element been more skilfully used than in "The Crier by Night." They have been used by Mr. Gordon Bottomley, whose play is the best piece of work that so far he has made public. . . . In this one-act play we have a greater advance than we dared to hope for, and we now venture to prophesy that Mr. Bottomley will, in the course of time, equal the finest work of our time. Even now the best passages of "The Crier by Night" have upon them that dew of magic that refreshes only the flowers of the true poet. We hope Mr. Bottomley's play will be put upon the stage ; but more than this, we hope that he will find another subject suited to his ability, and make of it a companion worthy to stand against this play upon our shelves.

SOME PRESS OPINIONS OF

The Morning Leader.

"The Crier by Night" has a haunting weirdness both in manner and plot, and the harmony is not broken by the passionate outbursts from its chief figure.

The Times Literary Supplement.

Mr. Gordon Bottomley, the author of "The Crier by Night," has much more of the poet in him; indeed, his little play, read in the study, is impressive.

The Week's Survey.

Mr. Gordon Bottomley has a feeling for stage-effect, and a certain impulse to work on broad and simple lines. We shall look with much interest to his future career. Dramatists who aspire to something better than the ordinary vulgarities and ineptitudes are still rare enough to deserve respect.

The late Dixon Scott, in *The Liverpool Courier.*

We have lamented again and again that the form of drama whose technique shall be made up of grave gestures, decorative backgrounds, long silent spaces, beautiful dances and music, and occasional rhythmical speech, is the form of drama which we most consistently ignore. . . . It finds a partial expression in Wagner, in M. Maeterlinck's "Death of Tintagiles," and perhaps in Mr. Gordon Bottomley's "Crier by Night"—although of this last it is as yet impossible adequately to judge, since the play remains astonishingly unacted.

The Daily Chronicle.

In "Midsummer Eve," as in his other poems, whether in lyric or dramatic form, he has gone to the deepest wells of his own personality, and though the draughts glimmer a little in the light of sun or moon or stars, they retain the incalculable and haunting gloom from which they came. . . . Almost as if he were bent on an extreme and glorious assertion of the poet's right to appear through his characters, as a strange and beautiful spirit sometimes appears through unpromising eyes and lips, so he makes the men and women of his play the medium for his expression of many of the moods which summer and night and rich landscapes, bringing many gifts, have brought to him. . . . And throughout the play the writer allows no conventions to deflect his purpose of expressing

MR. BOTTOMLEY'S PLAYS

midsummer nights as he has known them, and as he has pleased himself with dreaming that they may be in the unknown spirits of men and women who are part of them. Not that he neglects his characters, though he has hypnotized them, and filled them with his thought; they are, in fact, delicately distinguished; but he treats them, as everyone admits that Lancelot and Tristram and Palomides may be treated—as skeletons whom he must clothe with his own flesh. To everyone who acknowledges not only the legitimacy, but the naturalness, of such an attitude, the play will be a joy, Summer and Winter.

The Manchester Guardian.

In "Midsummer Eve" Mr. Gordon Bottomley has achieved a strange effect. His play treats of the primitive, very human superstition of ghosts. . . . The atmosphere of expectancy and excitement is well conveyed, nnd the externals—the bucolic environment and the hot scents of June—are caught with a certain conviction. . . . The farm-girls themselves are really far too profound philosophers for their business. . . . On the other hand, the more direct instincts of the sex are rather finely suggested.

The Academy.

"Midsummer Eve" is a dramatic poem with frequent passages of beauty. . . . An intangible warp on which to weave the texture of a poem. But the woven gossamer has parts so perfect that it is an impertinence to mention them with brevity.

Mr. Lascelles Abercrombie in *The Liverpool Courier*.

It would not be worth while drawing attention to "The Riding to Lithend," by Mr. Gordon Bottomley, if it belonged to the ordinary run of poetic drama whereof we see such plenty these days—in print; dramas, that is to say, which are laid out on the plan of a prose play, with a seasoning of poetry (or more probably of rhetoric) added in the speeches to give common fare a smart relish, like sponge-cake dipped in wine. But this is the sort of play for which many of us are looking, some consciously and some, perhaps more, unconsciously. . . . In these democratic days most modern works of art sit in the lower house; and they perform a very healthy office. But they must not pretend, however it may be in the corresponding political state of affairs, to the dignity and importance of those that are born to a seat in the upper house. Mr. Bottomley's "Riding to Lithend" is one of these latter. It is not a representative of life; it is a symbol of life. In it life is entirely fermented into rhythm, by which we mean not only rhythm of words, but rhythm of outline also ; the beauty and impressiveness of the play do not depend only on the subject, the diction, and the metre, but on the fact that it has distinct and most evident form, in the musician's sense of the word. It is one of those plays that reach the artist's ideal condition of music, in fact. . . .

It is constructed out of the elements of life, but those elements are built into a pattern according to the rhythmic laws of beauty, not according to the laws of verisimilitude ; and this it is, paradoxical as it may seem, that makes the existence Mr. Bottomley has contrived for his characters infect his readers with the sensation of an intenser actuality than is possible for any naturalism to achieve. . . .

The subject is stirring, and Mr. Bottomley takes it into a very high region of tragedy, giving it a purport beyond that of the original teller of the tale. But the events themselves of the play are so moving, the play itself leads up to the climax in such a forthright and exciting manner, that we cannot doubt that it would make a most powerful seizure on the attentions of an audience in the theatre. And a tragic actress would not have many such opportunities in the contemporary drama as is offered by the character of Hallgerd. This danger of a woman is perhaps the finest thing in the play. She is one who inhabits violence like an element. . . . There remains only the diction to be considered. Those who know Mr. Bottomley's previous work will be very ready to believe that it is fine, subtle, and distinguished ; and we may assure them that the poetry is stronger and more essential in this tragedy than in his earlier writings. The arresting epithet and the vivid strangeness of language are here ; but on the whole the poetry is of too stern a kind to need these decorations.

The format of the "Riding to Lithend" is beautiful and dignified. . . . We cannot help wondering whether, if Mr. Bottomley were less scrupulous in the production of his writings, he would not be better known. He is a poet who certainly ought to be much better known than he is. His play does not belong to any ordinary species of composition ; and it is the sort of tragedy that our stage needs perhaps more than anything else—if only our actor-managers could be persuaded of it.

" Iceland—and a Poet," by Mr. Arthur Waugh in *The Daily Chronicle*.

It is truly refreshing now and again, amid the dusty wilderness of verse-making, to come across a poem which is really

MR. BOTTOMLEY'S PLAYS

a poem. And this at least may be said, without fear, of Mr. Bottomley's haunting drama ; it is true poetry, true gold, ringing true with every echo. . . . It will be treasured and talked about by all the lovers of poetry for many years to come. . . . Like "The Haystack in the Floods," "The Riding to Lithend" is a deliberate attempt to picture an heroic age with the tinsel stripped from its garments ; to look primitive barbarism in the eyes without flinching. . . . Outside the poems of William Morris, the savagery of the heroic age has never, I think, been so wonderfully expressed. And it is to be noted that the most savage of all emotions come always from the women ; in the war-worn hero there is something of the weariness of Ulysses. . . . Whether this is true to history or not, I suppose none of us know—not even Mr. Bottomley himself. But he certainly contrives to make it appear inevitably real ; and that is all that criticism has a right to ask of poetry.

E. H. L. in *The Manchester Guardian.*

It is no small praise to say that the stirring Icelandic story of Gunnar loses nothing by Mr. Bottomley's telling. In his hands it has the quality of strong and deftly wrought metal, beaten and bright to catch the flame of some ancient, unspent, searing passion. . . . The atmosphere of doom and foreboding is set—admirably, classically—at the very start. . . . The poem moves evenly but swiftly to its issue. . . . Mr. Bottomley gives us these elemental things with extraordinary mastery, for that is the prevailing impression this poem leaves. It is all very simple and direct ; it is singularly free from artificiality of language and any effort to conjure up the archaic. . . . The verse is often, even in irregularity, musical. Proof as it is of a firmer touch, a surer control, this poem, luminous and so finely perceptive, must enhance a reputation that is already considerable.

The Bookman.

"The Riding to Lithend" is a drama of atmosphere—an atmosphere of doom that is over the play as a cloud. Its characters are marionettes dancing behind a curtain of grey gauze, shown up by flickering candle-light. . . . Mr. Bottomley is a poet. He writes blank verse which is vivid and supple and has a fine sense of the colour of words. Now and again he gets an absolutely Greek effect ; but there is little of the golden light of Greece about the play. It is a thing of gloom and fantastic shadows. . . . Poem and pictures alike show signs of growing on you.

SOME PRESS OPINIONS OF

"A New English Poet of Remarkable Power," by Mr. William Stanley Braithwaite in the *Boston (U.S.A.) Daily Transcript*.

"The Riding to Lithend" came to us as a seal of Mr. Bottomley's genius. . . . Among the many fine and rare things in British verse introduced to American readers, nothing has come for a long while in the field of poetic drama that is both so wholly unknown and of so exceptionally high an order. . . . Four of Mr. Bottomley's volumes are one-act plays in verse, and express his genius at its highest. . . . his natural poetic speech is through dramatic forms. . . . The most important are "The Crier by Night" and "The Riding to Lithend"; though we are inclined to think that the "Midsummer Eve" is a more balanced production, considered from all sides, than the others.

"The Crier by Night" invites comparison with the legendary and mystical poetic productions of the Celtic school; but there is none among them conceived on such sombre lines, nor fraught with such incisive and poignant sorcery. Its intensity is impressive with an atmosphere charged with electrified emotions. . . . In this play is brought out that quality in Mr. Bottomley's work which marks him apart from any poetic dramatist of his time . . . and it is a powerful and absorbing one. In "Midsummer Eve" he has achieved a surprising and beautiful piece of work . but what may be considered as his masterpiece, and one dares recommend it as such, is "The Riding to Lithend It is built upon firm, definite lines, and is vigorous with passion and character. . . . An effective element is the introduction of three beggar-women, whose speeches comprise some of the finest poetry in the piece. . . . Not often out of Shakespeare does one meet with a like success in the treatment of such unearthly beings.

I believe Mr. Bottomley is a poet whom English literature will come to regard in the possession of a power remarkable for its weight and conviction of human life in its sterner emotions beyond any contemporary poet; and who, as a dramatist, will present these emotions in character and action upon the stage in no distant future to the pulsation and surprise of human audiences.

Mr. Milton Bronner in *The Bookman* (New York.)

It seems to us that here is one of the most important of the younger poets, a writer who has studied and absorbed the culture of widely varied lands. . . . What makes these two poetic plays remarkable is not only their swift movement, their power

MR. BOTTOMLEY'S PLAYS

to induce an eerie feeling in the reader, their ability to set forth a character in a few lines, but also the verses themselves, sombre, drenched with melancholy, and displaying a uniform greyness of tone in keeping with the theme . . . stark lines that remind one of Rodin's sculptures. . . . In his remarkable one-act tragedy "The Riding to Lithend" he has done far more than tamely to copy the prose narrative of the saga. He has made a compact, high-strung, swiftly moving human tragedy out of an episode. He has taken the bare bones and clothed them with tragic beauty . . . and has made of Hallgerd an ardent Icelandic Helen instead of the lay figure the Saga for the most part depicts her. . . . He adds a very fine scene to the great fight with which in the main the saga story of Gunnar ends . . . a more human and pathetic note, one of the finest passages to be found in modern plays. . . It makes a wonderful impression upon the sympathetic reader ; and the same may be said of his other drama—"The Crier by Night."

Mr. S. P. B. Mais in *The Nineteenth Century and After*. On "Georgian Poetry," 1913-15.

It is impossible to re-read "King Lear" after finishing "King Lear's Wife" without noticing again and again points that used to puzzle the imagination, now made perfectly plain . . . an entirely new light on the relationship existing between Cordelia and her much older sisters . . . it helps us in our differentiation between Goneril and Regan . . . a blaze of sudden light thrown on Goneril as we have known her only in her later days. We gained some insight into Mr. Bottomley's poetic vision in the earlier volume of "Georgian Poetry"; but in "King Lear's Wife," he may, without hyperbole, be said to have arrived. Mr. Marsh is not wrong when he speaks of the honour which the author has done to the book by allowing his play to be published for the first time there. All readers at once feel impatient on coming to the end that they cannot at once rush out and see it acted. . . . Goneril's worship and lament are beautiful, not with an exotic richness that hides its meaning under a magic rhythm, but with the simplicity of Anglo-Saxon, monosyllabic yet haunting. Mr. Bottomley does not strive to heighten his effect by the introduction of the quaint or the remote : he is almost Blake-like in his choice of phrases. The result is that he has written a play which will remain in the memory as long as any we have ever read. It is a fine achievement; not the least fine part of its great attraction lying in that direct, straightforward simplicity.

219

SOME PRESS OPINIONS OF

Mr. Arthur Waugh in *The Daily Chronicle.*

To whatever school of poetry the reader may belong, he will hardly fail to be moved by the tragic vigour and genuine insight of "King Lear's Wife." . . . It certainly requires some confidence to add even a broken prelude to Shakespeare's acknowledged masterpiece. Yet Mr. Bottomley's courage may be held justified in the result, for he adds something definite to the popular picture of Lear. . . . It has just this essential amount of significance : no one who has once read it will ever read Shakespeare's " Lear" again without recalling Mr. Bottomley's gloss upon the manuscript. Whether that is justification or not may remain an open question. But it is certainly an achievement.

Professor C. H. Herford in *The Manchester Guardian.*

" King Lear's Wife," a remarkable dramatic piece, begins the volume. . . . Judged purely on its own merits, it has both beauty and dramatic power in no small degree.

The Times Literary Supplement.

We have enjoyed reading Mr. Bottomley's play . . we are interested in the setting out of his theme and in his considerable power of expressing himself . . . Mr. Bottomley shows what he can do with his character of Goneril. . . . The execution is vigorous with the energy of youth.

The Nation.

" King Lear's Wife" has distinction and felicity of phrasing.

The Spectator.

" King Lear's Wife " makes an appeal to ear and mind which is often extraordinarily attractive.　There is some really very powerful and very harmonious poetry developed in the telling of the story. . . . A word must be said about the wild beauty of some of Goneril's speeches. . . . Mr. Bottomley ought some day to do very fine work.

The Bookman.

Gordon Bottomley's remarkable poetic play, "King Lear's Wife," is full of passionate poetry. . . . His Goneril is really beautiful and most deeply felt. We feel her like a cold, pure wind in the book. Some of her passages are, indeed, worthy

MR. BOTTOMLEY'S PLAYS

of the Elizabethans. . . . Mr. Bottomley has a beautiful diction
. his poetry is noble, clean, plangent. There are so many
wonderful passages that one hardly knows which to choose.
. There is real enchantment in this poetry.

The Bookman. (Second notice.)

As a gloss on Shakespeare the play is valuable, and the
explanation—to us very necessary—of the aged king's harsh
reception by his two elder daughters is worked into a fine and
convincing drama.

Mr. W. L. Courtney in *The Daily Telegraph.*

Mr. Gordon Bottomley has written a powerful drama. The
piece is intensely vigorous, written in a nervous style, which
now and again attains to positive beauty.

Land and Water.

The description of Goneril moaning over her mother's death-
bed is clear and pellucid as crystal, magically arranged. . . .
The lines seem to have fallen into the speech as some of
Donne's lines fall—straight from heaven.

Colour.

The volume opens exceedingly well with Gordon Bottomley's
one-act play, " King Lear's Wife." This grips strongly, and is
live. . . . He has the precious gift of characterization ; his
people act as well as talk. . . . This grim little piece is not
made up, but born.

PERFORMANCES OF "THE CRIER BY NIGHT." The Portmanteau Theatre—Wyoming, Pittsburgh, Chicago, New York, U.S.A., 1916.

The New York Evening Telegram.

With the production of a poignant tragedy, Gordon
Bottomley's "The Crier by Night," Stuart Walker's Port-
manteau Theatre becomes a serious dramatic institution.

Chicago Daily Journal.

"The Crier by Night" is a Norse tragedy written with a
good deal of feeling for the thrilling word. . . . The speech is

·often richly patterned . . . there are many lines with music in them, and some with a thrill in them.

The Pittsburgh Sun.

" The Crier by Night " is sheer unrelaxed tragedy woven with an eerie mysticism suggestive of the Celtic. It moves inexorably by situations of increasing intensity to a climax that was the more concentrated because of the artistic harmony of acting, lighting, and setting with the spirit which pervades the piece. The lines are finely wrought poetry, and . . . they come convincingly from the lips of the characters as the natural expression of the tragedy of souls.

PERFORMANCES OF "KING LEAR'S WIFE."
Birmingham Repertory Theatre, 1915.
His Majesty's Theatre, London, 1916.

Birmingham Daily Post.

The personages have in them the stuff of life. . . . There is a stark power in this drama. . . . The Queen's spiritual desolation is piteous and beautiful . Nothing should blind us to the power and promise of the play.

Birmingham Evening Dispatch.

Let us say at once that here Mr. Bottomley has shown creative skill and dramatic power.

Birmingham Gazette.

Mr. Bottomley's play exhibits a large dramatic sense and a genuine command of literary graces in dialogue form.

The Observer. (London.)

Mr. Bottomley has beautiful ideas and beautiful poetry.

W. A. in The Star.

Mr. Bottomley's play is a powerfully conceived piece of ·drama.

The Manchester Guardian.

A play of strange vision and beauty. . . . The actor has a great opportunity for his vivid art in the middle-aged Lear of the play.

MR. BOTTOMLEY'S PLAYS

The Stage.

Mr. Bottomley shows imagination, a good deal of power of characterization, and an arresting gift of phrase.

Mr. Cecil Chisholm in *The Daily Chronicle.*

A relentless piece of realism. His verse is intensely dramatic. There is a brooding horror over " King Lear's Wife" that seems to be the very prelude to Shakespeare's searing tragedy.

Woven out of the rough stuff of life. .... Dramatic in a sense that the work of the great Victorians never could be.

Mr. Desmond MacCarthy in *The New Statesman.*

Mr. Bottomley's play has found many readers and many admirers. .... It held my attention in performance. .... In reading the play one is beguiled from noticing its emotional centre by the beauty of incidental passages. But on the stage it rises up, blocking out evanescent literary beauties. .... I noticed that the lines which told most on the stage were not those which I admired in reading the play. .... For instance, the passage in which Lear turns on Gormflaith was far more impressive than Goneril's much finer speech beginning " Through the waning darkness." The reader might pass over the former as an adequate bit of rhetoric and no more. Yet on the stage it had power and beauty; for it sprang direct from the emotion conveyed by the action at the moment. The body-washers' song was for some reason or other omitted : this was a pity. The gruesome and greedy indifference of the women was the right note to end on to wind up the tragedy of the queen.

LONDON: PRINTED AT THE CHISWICK PRESS
TOOKS COURT, CHANCERY LANE

Lightning Source UK Ltd.
Milton Keynes UK
UKHW02f1937230518
323110UK00035B/604/P